Before You Say I Don't

Before You Say I Don't

**A MANUAL FOR REVIVING YOUR MARRIAGE,
RESISTING DIVORCE, AND RESTORING HOPE**

Rick L. Goff

ISBN-13: 9781546873662
ISBN-10: 154687366X
Library of Congress Control Number: 2017908547
CreateSpace Independent Publishing Platform
North Charleston, South Carolina

Table of Contents

Dedication

It is only because of God's grace, love, and mercy, which were given to me through my Lord Jesus Christ, that I am even capable of writing this. If He is glorified in any way through this book, then I will be very pleased. God has blessed me in many ways, including blessing me with the absolute best wife I could have. Lori is not only my better half, but she does complete me. I know my security and identity is found in Christ, but she absolutely brings out my best, and worst, and yet loves me as I am.

Because of who she is, I am also so very blessed to have children who complete our family. Lori and I have been extremely honored to call Matt and his wife Cassie, Brittany and her husband Jon, Lindsey, and Andrew our children. And now as the family continues grow we are blessed with four wonderful grandchildren (Tucker, Brody, Gemma, Beckett). Yes, being a grandfather is totally amazing!

I also want to thank my own mom and dad, who for sixty-seven years didn't have a perfect marriage but demonstrated a commitment that overcame many obstacles. I know my dad would have been proud of this book if he were still with us today.

Lastly I am so thankful for my Faith Evangelical Free Church family and friends who have supported and encouraged me to stay the course in completing this book. I extend deep gratitude for the leadership at my church who gave me extended time to work on this book. I love all my family and friends for who they are in Christ!

Introduction

have been a pastor for over thirty years, including twenty-three years as a youth pastor, and in that time I have witnessed the joy and celebration of marriage and the hurt and turmoil of divorce. Divorce has become widely accepted in our culture, for a few possible reasons: (1) the 1985 adoption of no-fault divorce in all fifty states, (2) the moral decline of our nation, (3) the breakdown of the family, or (4) just a sign of the times. The growing acceptance of divorce has made it seem easier and acceptable for many couples when they face marital challenges, regardless of ethnicity, economic status, or religion. I have listened to people who having gone through a difficult divorce say, "If I could do it all over again, I would not have gone through with it." I have listened to and observed children of all ages who have been hindered or broken emotionally, socially, spiritually, or economically by divorce. Therefore, my hope is to encourage couples to slow down and think through the ramifications of a possible divorce before they say "I don't."

The purpose of this book is not to talk you into or out of divorce. This book is not intended to be a theological or biblical explanation of divorce. The purpose is to encourage couples to look at God's statement that "I hate divorce" (Malachi 2:16) and at least consider the reasons He said these three words.

Current estimates indicate that within five years following a divorce, about one-third of couples feel they made the right decision, another one-third are uncertain or have mixed feelings about their divorce, and approximately one-third of divorced couples regret the decision.[1]

In Minnesota, 66 percent of those who are currently divorced answered yes to the question "Do you wish you and your ex-spouse had tried harder to work through your differences?" In a New Jersey poll, 46 percent of divorced people reported that they wished they and their ex-spouse had tried harder to work through their differences. Research from Australia indicates that of people who divorce "one-third regret the decision five years later. Of the individuals involved, two in five (40 percent) believe their divorce could have been avoided."[2]

In my counseling work, I have observed that couples are not dealing with conflicts, sins, or communication issues when they arise. Therefore, they make the decision to divorce without weighing or knowing the consequences and damage that they and their family will face for years to come. Marital conflict and strife are not anything new, but having some possible solutions and a clearer understanding of those conflicts at least gives a clearer understanding of why God says, "I hate divorce." Hopefully, this can create a desire to fight for your marriage.

For those who have children, consider Jesus's words: "If one of these little children believes in me, and someone causes that child to sin, it would be better for that person to have a large stone tied around the neck and be drowned in the sea" (Matthew 18:6), and then later, "Let the little children come to me, and do not hinder them" (Matthew 19:14). I want to encourage you to at least pause and consider your responsibility to your children. Why? Because children matter to God. Your children matter to Him. God has given your children to you as a gift, and it is your responsibility to provide for, protect, and prepare them for the life they will face. How will divorce affect this precious gift? The Psalmist says, "Unless the LORD builds a house, the work of the builders is wasted. Children are a gift from the LORD; they are a reward from him" (Psalms 127:1, 3, NLT).

I ask you to prayerfully read through this book and take an insightful, thought- provoking, straight-forward, and honest look at making an intelligent and heartfelt decision about whether divorce is the best or wisest option for you.

Prepare Yourself for Marriage

Lori and I have been married for over thirty years, and before we were married our friend and pastor advised us to go through premarital counseling. It included exploring a book written by H. Norman Wright and Wes Roberts entitled *Before You Say "I Do": A Marriage Preparation Manual for Couples.*[3] Like most men I've counseled, I really didn't like going through premarital counseling, let alone going through a workbook. As I now look back, some thirty years later, I couldn't begin to tell you what was in that book, but I do know that it can help you think through the possibilities you might face. It can also begin to prepare you to face the life changes and challenges that "two becoming one" presents.

The workbook *Before You Say "I Do"* asks: "Would you like to have a successful, joyful marriage? Do you want to know more about your loved one's dreams and goals for your union?" Frankly, of the couples who come into my office or stand before me at the altar, I haven't encountered any who did not want to have a successful, joyful, and lasting marriage. Couples do not initially go into a marriage expecting to be miserable. They do not stand in their wedding attire looking forward to getting a divorce. However, the statistics indicate that divorce has affected over half of all marriages. Therefore, we must not only be prepared to have a healthy, lasting marriage, but *if* the time comes, then we must also be prepared to understand and think through the long-term ramifications of divorce.

Prepare Yourself for Divorce

Prepare yourself for divorce. Think about that: can you really honestly prepare yourself for divorce? You may not be able to prepare because of the many unknowns and because of the emotions you may or may not be able to control. But what you can prepare yourself for is a clearer and more insightful under-standing of some of the consequences if you pursue a divorce.

A familiar pattern I have noticed with couples considering getting a divorce is that they begin to struggle in their intimacy, in their communication, in their overall relationship, and without noticing it or acknowledging it, they begin to slowly grow apart. Couples do not understand or recognize that each step, each decision, and each day brings a greater risk of putting an end to the vows they took:

> "I, (your name), take thee, (insert your spouse name), to be my wedded husband/wife, to have and to hold, from this day forward, for better, for worse, for richer, for poorer, in sickness and in health, to love and to cherish, **until death do us part**, according to God's holy ordinance."

Typically, one or both spouses know or *feel* something is wrong, but they choose not to take any steps to change, address, or improve their situation. Research shows that, on average, people wait six years before seeking marriage therapy. Way too many couples never receive help and end up running right over to a divorce attorney's office to begin a process that will drastically impact everyday decisions and logistics for the rest of their lives.

Below are just a few consequences for those who have traveled the road of divorce. As you think about your own situation, try to answer the following questions:

- Am I ready for the fact that my household income will likely be cut in half? Am I ready to live below poverty level?
- When I observe divorced persons, does it seem their problems are resolved when they find someone new? Or does partnering with someone new only double their trouble?"
- Will the children be better off, or will they be torn in two by not having one place to call home, going back and forth every week between the two parents?
- When I remarry, what set of grandparents will my children invite to grandparents' day in grade school?
- Will I now have to compete with my ex on buying the best Christmas gift for our children?
- If my daughter grows up liking her stepfather better than me, will she ask him, rather than me, to walk her down the aisle when she gets married?
- Will my children have to separate their parents on their wedding day because we can't get along? (Unfortunately, I have seen this many, many times, and it is ugly!)
- Will I always feel insecure by comparing myself with my ex's new spouse?
- How many Thanksgivings or Christmas days will I be alone while my children visit my ex?

Through his puppet, Walter, comedian/ventriloquist Jeff Dunham jokes, "I didn't know 'till death do us part' became a goal." I have heard spouses and children who have gone through a divorce describe it as a death in the family. These are valid questions we must ask to begin to understand the real pain couples experience when they go through with a divorce.

If you are on the verge of divorce, my hope and prayer is that you will at least consider the ramifications for the life you will face if you choose to proceed with splitting up your family. Realize that the pain may be even greater than you feel you are going through right now. The stakes are high—really high—and making a wise, informed decision is the best route you can take.

God created marriage for "the two [to] become one flesh." When you join in marriage and consummate the union, a soul bond is created. Adam said, "This is now bone of my bone and flesh of my flesh."

The two become one. Have you ever tried to separate two objects that were glued together? When you do so, you find that the bond holding the two objects together makes it nearly impossible to separate them without causing damage to both sides. That's the picture of divorce. Divorce is a tearing apart, and it is damaging emotionally, socially, relationally, economically, and psychologically.

Marriage is not a causal relationship that can be discarded with "no fault." Spouses shouldn't say "I don't" or "I'm done" without knowing all the facts about where they are and where they are headed for the rest of their life. This life-changing decision will disrupt their future, their finances, their children, their emotions, their social circles, and their spiritual well-being. Family members will be affected to some degree, creating a chain reaction that will impact family decisions and outside relationships for years to come.

Whether to divorce or work on the marriage and remain together is one of the most important decisions you will make at this critical time in your life. While advocating marriage, I do want to be sensitive to those who have chosen to terminate their marriage.

In *The Meaning of Marriage*, Timothy Keller says,

> Divorce should not be easy; it should not be our first, second, third, or fourth resort. And yet, Jesus knows the depths of human sin and holds out hope for those who find themselves married to someone with an intractably hard heart who has broken his or her vow. Divorce is terribly difficult, and it should be, but the wronged party should not live in shame. Surprisingly, even God claims to have gone through a divorce (Jeremiah 3:8). He knows what it is like.[4]

There are legitimate reasons or grounds for divorce. An estimated 30 percent of the divorces in the United States occur in marital relationships with a high degree of conflict. Sometimes violence, physical and mental abuse, or threats to the lives of the spouse and children are also present in these high-conflict relationships. In such situations, divorce is most often in the best interest of those involved.[5]

Think about what can happen to families if even some of the remaining 70 percent of marriages can begin to heal the hurt. I am going to ask you to take an honest look and ask if your marriage can be improved and saved from divorce before you say "I don't." If you and your spouse are still together,

you have hope. Things are possible; Jesus said, "With man this is impossible, but not with God; all things are possible with God" (Mark 10:27). Do not underestimate what God can and will do in your life, your marriage, and your family. As you know, there are more books, papers, and blogs dealing with marriage and divorce than anyone could ever read. Maybe you won't find anything new in these pages beyond what the experts have already said, but I do hope that you would seriously and prayerfully consider why God says, "I hate divorce." If your marriage is struggling but has not yet failed, then you still have time to repair what you started with your spouse.

I will begin every chapter with a funny story. Most of us know from experience that having a sense of humor can make life a little easier. Humor has also been identified as a possible factor in developing personal resilience. "If you can laugh at yourself, you can forgive yourself, and if you can forgive yourself, you can forgive others," says Susan Sparks, author of *Laugh Your Way to Grace*.[6] We need to be able to laugh about where we are and who we are. Mark Twain said, "The human race has only one really effective weapon, and that is laughter."[7] The benefits of laughter can be instantaneous. There's a great deal of evidence that laughing improves both our mental and physical health. Begin with an open heart and mind and a hope that God will restore joy in your heart and marriage.

CHAPTER 1

First Things First

> "The first bond of society is marriage."
> ROMAN STATESMAN AND ORATOR MARCUS TULLIUS CICERO (106–43 BC)

Comedian Ken Davis tells this joke: A forty-five-year-old man pulls out of a Minnesota car dealer's parking lot in his new Corvette. He squeals the tires, and within no time has the car up to seventy, eighty, ninety miles per hour. He gets out into the open road, where he hits a hundred, and then he sees lights in his rearview mirror. He tries to get away, getting up to 150 mph, until he realizes it's not worth it, so he pulls over.

The state trooper comes up to the window and says, "There's five minutes left on my shift, and it's Friday, and I have the weekend off. If you can give me an excuse that I've never heard before, I'll let you off without a ticket."

The man looks at him and says, "Twenty years ago this week, my wife ran off with a Minnesota State Trooper, and I was afraid you were bringing her back."

Trooper says, "Have a great weekend" and walks away.

We have all heard or repeated jokes about marriage or being married—and quite honestly, some of them are very funny. Unfortunately, when it comes to marriage and divorce, the saying "it's so sad it's funny" really holds true. I want you to think back to your wedding day and remember the laughter, fun, and joy that filled that event. As I stated before, couples do not go into marriage being miserable or thinking they'll be the ones who won't make it. Certainly, at your wedding, you thought you were promising a love that would last a lifetime. There was joy in your heart, and there is a reason you married in the first place.

First Impressions

Research indicates that you may only get a few seconds to make a first impression that is tied to the future of your relationship.[8] Marriages are made for life, but first impressions take place within the first few moments of meeting someone—and they can last a lifetime. Those few moments are all the time you have to make a powerful first impression on your future spouse.

We must understand that the past, both good and bad, make us who we are today and influence how we react to the present. But remember that it can be mentally and relationally dangerous to stay or live in the past too long because then we can often miss how to deal with the present.

So, what was it for you? What were some of the firsts with your spouse that led you to becoming husband and wife? It is important for us to remember the thrill of the first time for anything in life. I want you to think about some of your favorite firsts:

- Where was your first kiss?
- What happened the first time your eyes met?
- Where was your first date?
- What emotions drove you toward each other?
- What did you feel the first time your hands touched?
- Was it love at first sight when you first met?
- What was the first song you remember as *your* song?
- What was your honeymoon or first family vacation like?
- What went through your mind when you found out you were having a baby or the first time you saw your children after they were born?
- What was it that first brought the two of you together?
- What interests or likes and dislikes did you have?
- What do you remember about the first time you were intimate?

Instead of just remembering those first impressions, how exciting it would be if you could relive or reenact that time again as if it were the first time. Think about all that you valued together in your life, and then begin to act as if you could experience them once more...for the first time. After all, that's where it all started; that's why you got married in the first place. If you don't think being reminded about the first times can make a difference, then you don't understand what is happening with social media, specifically Facebook. A limited study of 5,436 divorce cases by a law firm found that around 20 percent of divorce filings mentioned the popular social networking site Facebook; people are going back to their first loves, their first boyfriend or girlfriend.[9]

If you have not seen the movie *Fireproof*, then I encourage you to take time to watch it with your spouse.[10] In this movie, a couple dares to rescue their choking marriage from the flames of divorce and temptation using the book *The Love Dare* as a guide. In one scene, Kirk Cameron's character says to his wife, "God has given me a love for you that I've never had before." The "Love Dare" introduced in this movie is a great devotional that helps couples prioritize first things first. Nearly every marriage has something worth preserving, something that can be restored. Restoring a relationship brings hope, joy, and triumph and can provide ongoing rewards. Bringing back that loving feeling (more about love in chapter 4) and avoiding divorce spares everyone from one of the greatest traumas of their life.

YOU NEVER LEAVE YOUR PARTNER
ESPECIALLY DURING A FIRE

First Marriage

One of my favorite duties as a pastor is meeting with couples for premarital counseling, and then performing the wedding ceremony itself. It is or should be a tremendously joyful and unforgettable day for the couple. Marriage is a divine institution that was established in the very beginning. If our first impression about marriage is in line with God's desire for the very first marriage, then we will begin to appreciate and understand what our marriage can become.

> Then God said, "Let us make man in our image, in our likeness, and let them rule over the fish of the sea and the birds of the air, over the livestock, over all the earth, and over all the creatures that move along the ground." So God created man in his own image, in the image of God he created him; male and female he created them. God blessed them and said to them, "Be fruitful and increase in number; fill the earth and subdue it. Rule over the fish of the sea and the birds of the air and over every living creature that moves on the ground" (Genesis 1:26–28).

Before there was sin, there was marriage. Marriage was put in a sinless environment created by God. God said it. God created it. Then, God blessed it. Marriage is a divine institution. It is God's idea, not man's idea. We must not lose sight of that truth, because it reveals that the marriage covenant comes directly from God Himself. He sanctioned it, and He can sustain it if you allow Him to. Marriage was created to be the most rewarding of all human relationships, and it can transform you if you understand and stand on the promise of God and His covenant. Only in the last several years, after being reminded through God's Word and reading several books, I came to realize just how important it is to know and understand God's covenant in marriage. This is one reason I have become even more passionate about encouraging couples to stick to their marriage vows.

According to writer Tony Evans,

> What married couples often want to do is to have God's institution of marriage, yet run it by their own rules. They want to get married in the church so that God will bless their marriage, but then they want to leave God standing at the altar. They want to make up their own rules for how a marriage should be run...Let me tell you a secret. Pay attention: You don't get God's results without operating by God's rules. You don't get God's blessings in your marriage and in your home without following God's instructions. You don't enjoy God's provision, protection and peace in your relationships without abiding by God's policies concerning the covenantal union of marriage.[11]

It is important to understand that in your marriage, your problem is not you against each other; it's you two against the world. Marriage takes work, and at times it will be a battle, but it is important to know that battle is not you against your spouse. It's a war against our sin nature.[12] Every marriage has both an earthly and a spiritual enemy we need to be aware of: the self and Satan. One mighty opponent that can be easily identified is named selfishness. If we are honest about our marriage issues, the problem usually comes down to "what I want." Think about most disagreements that come up in all marriages: money, children, recreation, future, career, etc. The argument usually centers around wanting it "my way," with little to no regard of what is best for others.

In addition to selfishness, another enemy of our marriages is Satan. Scripture makes it clear that Satan is the god of this world (2 Corinthians 4:4), because he knows that your marriage could be used for God's kingdom, and Satan fears that. Thus, he works tirelessly to destroy Christian marriages. The enemy can be seen working through our government in establishing the no-fault divorce law and tax credits that make it easier to cohabitate than to get married. As the father of lies, the devil is real, and he wants to destroy not only our individual lives, but God's institution of marriage and family (John 8:44). The Apostle Paul says our battle is not against people, but against the powers of evil (Ephesians 6:12). Because every marriage has two enemies, selfishness and Satan, it's essential that couples stay engaged in the battle for a thriving marriage.

Since the fall of man, we have seen how humanity has a tendency to live for self. Selfishness is part of our DNA. The "me first" attitude has significantly impacted the commitment to "until death do us part" in our culture today, and that vow is viewed drastically differently than it was just ten, twenty, or thirty years ago.

God's plan all along was for the essence and joy of marriage to be a sacrificial commitment to the good of the other. Jesus said, "The two will become one flesh. So they are no longer two, but one" (Mark 10:8). That oneness was perfectly demonstrated in Christ's life and death for His bride, the Church. Jesus's life and death was all about you! He put you and your interests before His own, and that is how God desires us to live our life together…"happily ever after."

The Apostle Paul reminds us about what is important to remember in all of our relationships:

Do nothing out of selfish ambition or vain conceit, but in humility consider others better than yourselves. Each of you should look not only to your own interests, but also to the interests of others. Your attitude should be the same as that of Christ Jesus (Philippians 2:3–5).

Putting others before your own interests can drastically change the marriage relationship and will bring us in line with God's desire for marriage to be a covenant relationship.

Timothy Keller says,

Contemporary Western societies make the individual's happiness the ultimate value, and so marriage becomes primarily the experience of romantic fulfillment. But the Bible sees God as the supreme good—not the individual or the family—and that gives us a view of marriage that intimately unites feeling *and* duty, passion *and* promise. That is because at the heart of the Biblical idea of marriage is the covenant.

In the Biblical covenant, the good of the relationship takes precedence over the immediate needs of the individual. The concept of a covenant is tremendously foreign to us, and yet it is the essence of marriage. Therefore, it is important to know what it is. It is because of this covenant that God hates divorce:

> You ask, "Why?" It is because the LORD is acting as the witness between you and the wife of your youth, because you have broken faith with her, though she is your partner, the wife of your marriage covenant. Has not [the LORD] made them one? In flesh and spirit they are His. And why one? Because he was seeking godly offspring. So guard yourself in your spirit, and do not break faith with the wife of your youth. "I hate divorce," says the LORD God of Israel (Malachi 2:14–16)

The marriage relationship is a covenant unlike any other relationship. It is a union designed to strengthen the capability of each partner to carry out God's plan in their lives. That's why your marriage matters! That's why it is worth the time and effort, the hurt and pain to seek what's best for your marriage.

There is a story about a boy who lost one of his contact lenses. He spent a significant amount of time trying to locate it, but he couldn't find it. He finally reluctantly told his mom. They boy's mom began looking for the contact lens with him and found it in only a matter of minutes. The surprised boy asked, "How could you find that in just a few minutes when I have been looking for a while?" The mom replied, "That's easy. You didn't find it because you were looking for a contact lens. I found it because I was looking for two hundred fifty dollars."

Can find what you're looking for in your marriage? It depends on what you are looking for. Is your marriage struggling or on the edge of divorce because you have lost sight of the purpose or because you fail to understand the richness of the marriage covenant? God's covenant to us, and our covenant to our marriage, can make all the difference in the world!

According to S. Michael Craven,

> The marriage covenant is singularly unique in civilization; it is not simply a civil or romantic union between two people. Rather, it is an emotional, physical, and spiritual union between one man and one woman. It is emotional in the sense that two people, male and female, each with different (complementary) attributes, join together in life, assisting one another, nurturing and caring for one another, and affirming and guiding one another—in essence, completing the other. It is physical in the sense that marriage is procreative. Two separate biological beings blend together to create what neither can create on their own: children. And lastly, marriage is spiritual in the sense that we are made for this partnership that places the interest of the other (or others, in the case of children) above self—a relationship that ultimately mirrors God's sacrificial love toward each of us and His bride: the church.[13]

Understanding what God says about marriage and the covenant promise you made to Him will help you understand that God can heal a broken marriage. Not understanding or losing sight of the marriage covenant is one of the reasons cohabitation has compromised biblical marriage. Marriage is so much more than a civil union; it's a commitment to complete each other. Take time to think about that statement: *Your marriage is a commitment to complete each other.* Think about how that commitment can drastically change your heart and attitude. That alone is one of many reasons why cohabitation falls short of God's desire for man and woman to become one. Cohabitation means there are no strings attached, no commitment to the good or well-being of the other person. There may be some reasonable motives for living together, but generally it is to protect one's own personal finances or future assets. That was not and is not God's plan or desire for two to become one. Biblically, a covenant is a spiritually binding relationship between God and His children, inclusive of any agreements, conditions, benefits, and effects. Imagine if that was how we began to deal with our marriages despite any differences, disagreements, and difficult circumstances.

First Step

Think about any first steps you have experienced or witnessed in your life. Many situations could qualify, but the one that stands out is watching my children take their first steps. As parents, we look forward to many different stages in our children's lives, but the moment they let go and take a step seems to be a big one. Whether it's because it signals a new beginning, a new freedom (both for you and them), or literally a new step in life, it really can be an exciting moment.

As you think about your own marriage and God's plan for you, what will it take for you to hold onto the marriage covenant that you established before God and with your spouse? It will require a willingness to take a first step. The steps you take are always important, because they will move you forward. The alternative is choosing to not take a step and stay right where you are. That is called stagnation, and it is never a good alternative. Doing the same thing over and over again means you will keep getting the same results. Is that really what you want? Standing still or doing nothing in your marriage is not an option. In a 1981 Narcotics Anonymous text that has at times been attributed to Albert Einstein is: "The definition of insanity is doing the same thing over and over again but expecting different results."

The first few steps you take on any journey won't get you where you want to go, but without those first steps you will always be standing right where you are, looking toward the future, wondering what happened, and thinking, "How did I get here?" One of the greatest lessons in life is learning from experience and moving forward. I have coached high-school track and cross-country for over twenty-five years. For the most part, every year we start at square one. It is always fun and exciting to watch young men and women take that first step that ultimately can lead them to standing on the podium at the state meet. I am fortunate enough to have coached some state champions, but I am just as proud of those who came with very little or no confidence in their running capabilities only to achieve success to any degree. Regardless of talent, each individual had to take that first step. It is a must!

Jesus reminds us about taking the first step in our relationship with Him: "But I have this against you: You have left the love you had in the beginning. So remember where you were before you fell. Change your hearts and do what you did at first" (Revelation 2:4, NCV). Jesus asks us to evaluate and see if we have lost our love for Him. Why? Because it is easy to lose our focus on what is really important. He says we need to be intentional and open to changing our heart; we need to do what we did at first in our relationship. Specifically, think about your spouse and consider what steps you might need to take that will fit the interests, values, and life you want to lead together. Taking steps forward and reflecting on the value of attaining your goal can help you commit—and recommit—to each other. This is what makes our first step so important. The first step marks a decision, a new direction; it declares that we will go forward despite our fears or self-doubt. The first step gives us momentum and belief in our relationship. For some, the first step might be to acknowledge that there is a problem and you need to begin to do something— now. Realize that it wasn't *just* one step that got you where you are today, but it did take that first step of neglect, poor communication, self-centeredness, or sin to move you and your spouse apart.

It will certainly take more than one step to move where you want your relationship to go, but you must take that step. And it's one step worth taking: a step in the right direction.

First Priority of a Nation

Marriage not only impacts the couple when the "two become one flesh," but it also has a tremendous impact on a nation. Professor and President of Probe Ministries Kerby Anderson writes, "Nations most often fall from within and this fall is usually due to a decline in the moral and spiritual values in the family. As families go, so goes a nation."[14] This is the main premise of historians who study civilizations that have collapsed. That is how important your marriage and your family's stability is! Families are the foundation of a nation, and when the family crumbles the nation falls, because nations are built upon family units. They are the true driving social force. A nation will not be strong unless the family is strong. Social commentator Michael Novak, writing on the importance of the family, says: "One unforgettable law has been learned through all the disasters and injustices of the last thousand years: If things go well with the family, life is worth living; when the family falters, life falls apart."[15]

In Anderson's paper, he states that each of the great civilizations in the world passed through a series of stages, from birth to decline to death. Here are the stages:

1. **Men ceased to lead their families in worship**. Spiritual and moral development became secondary. Their view of God became naturalistic, mathematical, and mechanical.
2. **Men selfishly neglected care of their wives and children** to pursue material wealth, political and military power and cultural development. Material values began to dominate thought and the man began to exalt his own role as an individual.
3. **A change in men's sexual values**. Men who were preoccupied with business or war either neglected their wives sexually or became involved with lower-class women or with homosexuality. Ultimately, a double standard of morality developed.
4. **Affected women**. The role of women at home and with children lost value and status. Women were neglected and their roles devalued. Soon they revolted to gain access to material wealth and also freedom for sex outside marriage. Women also began to minimize having sex relations to conceive children and the emphasis became sex for pleasure. *Marriage laws were changed to make divorce easy.* (My emphasis)
5. **Husbands and wives competed against each other** for money, home leadership and the affection of their children. This resulted in hostility and frustration and possible homosexuality in

the children. *Many marriages ended in separation and divorce.* Many children were unwanted, aborted, abandoned, molested and undisciplined. The more undisciplined children became, the more social pressure there was not to have children. The breakdown of the home-produced anarchy.

6. **Selfish individualism grew and carried over into society**, fragmenting it into smaller and smaller group loyalties. The nation was thus weakened by internal conflict. The decrease in the birthrate produced an older population that had less ability to defend itself and less will to do so, making the nation more vulnerable to its enemies.

7. **Unbelief in God became more complete**, parental authority diminished and ethical and moral principles disappeared, affecting the economy and government. Thus, by internal weakness and fragmentation the societies came apart.[16]

> If things go well with the family, life is worth living; when the family falters, life falls apart.

In our own upbringing, we all have been personally affected by at least one of the stages listed above. It is important to understand that your marriage or divorce impact not only your life and your family, but also our nation and the direction it's headed.

Do not underestimate the impact of the decisions you will make in regard to your marriage. If we cannot learn from our own mistakes and the mistakes of others, then we will repeat them. The philosopher and poet George Santayana said, "Those who forget the past are condemned to repeat it." Think about how many times you have said or heard others say "It won't happen to me" only to watch it happen?

History has shown that the average age of great civilizations is around two hundred years. Countries like Great Britain exceed the average, while other countries like the United States are just now reaching the average age. This is not like the boy crying wolf or a prophet on the street corner warning that the end is near. It is taking an honest and open look around us, seeing where we are and where we are heading individually and collectively.

Several researchers and authors have reported the importance of a stable marriage. In his book *Why Marriage Matters*, Glenn T. Stanton writes:

As the researchers have gone to press with their work and produced an enormous literature, one of the most consistent findings is that men and women do markedly better in all measures of specific and general well-being when they are married, compared to any of their unmarried counterparts. Married couples are healthier—physically and mentally—and they live longer, enjoy a more fulfilled life, and take better care of themselves (and each other). This has been shown consistently over decades, but it is rarely mentioned in the popular debate on the family. One of social science's best-kept secrets is that marriage is much more than a legal agreement between two people. Marriage truly makes a difference in the lives of men and women.[17]

> **One of social science's best-kept secrets is that marriage is much more than a legal agreement between two people. Marriage truly makes a difference in the lives of men and women.**

What is your family history when it comes to marriage and divorce? In your own life, how have you personally been impacted by your parents and their relationship? What hope do your children have as a result of your marriage staying together? Is your marriage at all worth fighting for? Only you can answer these questions, and only you can make a difference in your marriage, but you must be willing to take the first step and begin to restore the love and life that you first desired—and that God still desires for you.

Recounting Real Relationships

Following every chapter, I will share true stories from people who I have known and counseled through the years. These people who have gone through a variety of experiences when it comes to marriage and divorce. I have left out names at the request of those who wrote the stories except for the one that was previously published elsewhere.

The first Recount Real Relationship story we will look at will be my own. As I mentioned before, Lori and I have been married for over thirty years. It truly is only by the grace of God that we are where we are today. That's not because something bad happened or our marriage has been bad, but because, as in all marriages, it has taken a lot of work, prayer, and faith to successfully stay together. Like most, if not all, couples, Lori and I both come from dysfunctional families, each with a variety of different dysfunctions. Lori comes from a Christian family, and I didn't. We both have family issues and baggage we have had to deal with.

Lori and I are thankful that we both came from families where there was no divorce going back several generations. My own parents were married for over sixty years until my dad recently passed away. Both sets of my grandparents were married more than fifty-five or sixty years. Lori's parents are going on their fifty-seventh year of marriage, and both of her grandparents were also married over fifty-five years. Obviously, such a history of marriage with no divorce is not a guarantee of staying together, as is evidenced by some of our own siblings going through divorces. However, we were free of any negative experience of divorce in our own families, thus bringing that mind-set into our own marriage.

We would like to think that being Christ followers and me being a pastor for the past thirty years has helped keep us together, but we know that Christians are getting divorced at the same rate as anyone else. And unfortunately, pastors are not exempt from divorce either. Since I began writing this book, I personally have become aware of at least six pastors, including a very close friend, who have gone through divorce. In my marriage, did our faith and desire to follow and please God help? Absolutely, but there is so much more than that.

Lori and I both have our warts, sins, and personal baggage, but I believe we are together because God is good all the time and we never contemplated divorce as an option. Our children never heard us so much as mention divorce as a possibility, even during those times of heated exchanges. Has marriage been easy? No! Are we patting ourselves on the back? No, because we know it wasn't and isn't about us. The success of our marriage really is due to a wide variety of reasons, and in chapter 6 I list twelve basic principles that helped us over our thirty years. There are obviously many, many more principles that have added to the joy, fun, and blessings of being together and staying together.

The phrase "Life is hard; it's harder if you're stupid" could be applicable in the area of marriage and divorce. Marriage will be hard, and it does take work. I have witnessed too many failed marriages that have seemed to have just withered and died from a lack of effort. God made it clear that marriages don't fail—humans do! But just because too many have failed to live up to God's ideal of marriage, and just because the institution of marriage is under pressure, doesn't mean it's impossible to build a marriage that is a safe haven of peace, love, and inspiration. As wise King Solomon told his son, "A man's greatest treasure is his wife—she is a gift from the Lord" (Proverbs 18:22, CEV).

There is no magic pill or formula that guarantee a long, lasting, and healthy marriage. I remember early on in dating, Lori and I individually came to the same conclusion: that God had brought us together. In our own personal faith journey, we know that God doesn't make mistakes. How much has our faith in Christ helped our relationship? I don't really know, except to say: a lot! How much does our personalities help keep us together? Well, at times they help, and at times they make things difficult! How much will our own children benefit from us staying together? I really don't know, but we are so very thankful we did! Will it help them? Only as much as they allow it to make a difference in their own families. There are no magic pills. God's grace and love works in and through us. The treasure in marriage is the loving, stable environment that provides secure, lifelong emotional bonds and nurtures children, who carry forward positive contributions to society. Both Lori and I definitely agree with the quote below about being two imperfect people who not only have learned the value of forgiveness and grace, but realize the need to extend it and receive it time and time again over the last thirty-two years has been crucial.

> "A successful marriage isn't the union of two perfect people. It's that of two imperfect people who have learned the value of forgiveness and grace."[18]
> DARLENE SCHACHT

Journey Together
Marriage Workbook

1) To put "First Things First," as this chapter is titled, decide together that you desire to work through this book. Set up a specific day(s) and time that you will commit to it. During your first session together, go back and look at the pictures of your wedding or watch the DVD of that special day.

Day: _____

Time: _____

Signature (this shows you are serious):

_____,   _____
                    Wife   Husband

2) On a scale of 1–10 (10 being great), where is your marriage right now? What would your spouse say? Why did you indicate this number? How do you think it can improve with God's help?

_____

_____

_____

3) Go back to the list of questions about remembering some of your first impressions about your spouse. Pick out and list three to five that stand out for you.

Wife   Husband

_____   _____

_____   _____

_____   _____

_____   _____

_____   _____

4) Together, choose one item from the list in the question above that you choose to focus on rekindling. Think about specific ways you will go about accomplishing them and decide when you will begin this process. This may stretch you and therefore you may have to get out of your comfort zone but it will be well worth the extra effort to accomplish it.

_____

_____

_____

5) Schedule a date night to watch the movie *Fireproof*, just the two of you. As a follow-up, purchase *The Love Dare* study guide.[19]

6) It was stated that every marriage has two enemies, selfishness and Satan. Think about how you might stay engaged in the battle to have a thriving marriage. Here are some practical ways you can declare open war against evil in your marriage:

   - If you are too busy, consider which activities you can give up to strengthen your marriage.
   - Remember, it is a spiritual battle. Husbands, take the lead in setting aside time for daily prayer and reading with your wife. Discuss how you and your family can connect to God. Some examples could include going on a family vacation, spending time outdoors, or volunteering in your community or at church.
   - Maintain a healthy devotion time with God so He can show you where you need to grow.
   - Repent of and abandon any sin in your life.
   - If your spouse is feeling ignored or overlooked, put his or her interest above your own. Invest some time in pleasing your spouse.
   - Open your heart and spirit to God. This will help both of you be better able to resolve conflict.

---

7) Read the following verses and discuss how selfishness can hinder our relationship and ways to overcome being selfish:

   - Philippians 2:3–4
   - James 3:16
   - 2 Timothy 3:1–2
   - James 3:14–16
   - Colossians 3:13–14

---

8) What does it mean to you that your marriage is a covenant established by God? How does that affect your thinking when it comes to commitment and/or divorce?

_____

_____

_____

9) Go back in this chapter and look at the list of the stages that civilizations go through. Identify one or two of them that you believe might have influenced where you are today in your marriage. Answer the following questions in light of this list:
   - Where is our country in regard to marriage, divorce, or family breakdown?
   - Do you see our own country following suit with the collapse of a nation because of marriages failing?
   - Are there patterns in your family history that are adding to the decline of our nation?
   - Are you prepared to be part of the problem or the solution? The only person who can change the course of our history is _you_.
   - Are you willing to change the course of history, including your own family history?
   - What will the next generation, or your children, learn from **you** and how you deal with conflict and difficulties in marriage?

_____

_____

_____

10) One very important and specific step you can take regularly, every day, in every conflict, and in every disagreement is to pray. Prayer may not always change your situation, but it can change you and your heart. If you are looking for prayers for your marriage visit my website, www.beforeisayno. com.

_____

_____

_____

PRAY TOGETHER

Here is a prayer to get you started, and remember: it's not the words that matter so much as what's in your heart. Read it out loud:

Dear Heavenly Father, I know that You are always here and present in my life. You are the only all-knowing, all-powerful, ever-present God. I desperately need You, because without Jesus I can do nothing. I believe the Bible because it is the absolute truth, and I desire to follow Your Word. I refuse to believe the lies of Satan. I stand in the truth that all authority in heaven and on earth has been given to the resurrected Christ. I ask you to protect my thoughts and mind and lead me into all truth. I choose to submit to the Holy Spirit and His leading in my marriage. Please reveal to my mind everything You want to deal with. I ask for and trust in Your wisdom. I pray for Your complete protection over me, my spouse, and my family. In Jesus's Name, Amen

CHAPTER 2

Facts and Nothing but the Facts

*"People will generally accept facts as truth only if
the facts agree with what they already believe."*
ANDY ROONEY

There is a story about a big-city California lawyer who went duck hunting in rural Texas. He shot and dropped a bird, but it fell into a farmer's field on the other side of a fence. As the lawyer climbed over the fence, an elderly farmer drove up on a tractor and asked him what he was doing. The litigator responded, "I shot a duck, and it fell in this field, and now I'm going in to retrieve it."

The old farmer replied. "This is my property, and you are not coming over here."

The indignant lawyer said, "I am one of the best trial attorneys in the United States, and if you don't let me get that duck, I'll sue you and take everything you own."

The old farmer smiled and said, "Apparently, you don't know how we do things in Texas. We settle small disagreements like this with the Texas Three-Kick Rule."

The lawyer asked, "What is the Texas Three-Kick Rule?"

The farmer replied, "Well, first I kick you three times, and then you kick me three times, and so on, back and forth, until someone gives up."

The attorney quickly thought about the proposed contest and decided that he could easily take the old codger. He agreed to abide by the local custom.

The old farmer slowly climbed down from the tractor and walked up to the city feller. His first kick planted the toe of his heavy work boot into the lawyer's groin and dropped him to his knees. His second kick landed square on the man's nose. The barrister was flat on his belly when the farmer's third kick to a kidney nearly caused him to give up.

The lawyer summoned every bit of his will and managed to get to his feet and said, "Okay, you old coot, now it's my turn!"

The old farmer smiled and said, "Naw, I give up. You can have the duck."

It is obvious that this lawyer should have known all the facts before he agreed to this contest. Having all the facts is important when it comes to marriage and divorce especially when it is becoming increasingly evident to those to those who study marriage trends in the United States, that a large number of divorces could, and perhaps should, be avoided in the best interests of those involved.[20]

Think about Mr. Rooney's quote in view of your own life. Do you see that it's true for you? Do you see that's the case for others? A fact is understood to be a statement that can be proven true or false, whereas an opinion is an expression of a person's feelings and cannot be proven. Opinions can be based on facts or emotions, and sometimes they can be hard to separate and figure out. In the last chapter, we looked at what we should have learned from history. In chapter 3 we will look at how we can better understand and separate our feelings and emotions when determining our future. Therefore, in this chapter we will bridge the gap with a look at some facts and statistics about divorce and its potential consequences.

Divorce and the process leading up to it can be an extremely volatile, emotional time, and therefore knowing how it has affected those who have walked in those shoes can help separate facts from feelings. Scott Young said, "Having factual knowledge matters because it determines the speed you can acquire new knowledge on any given topic. The more you know, the faster you learn and hopefully are willing to change."[21] What we find on the Internet today through Google, Facebook, Twitter, YouTube, or *Wikipedia* does not remove the burden of learning factual knowledge; it actually increases the importance of learning. When we use these resources as an excuse not to learn, we won't just be ignorant of the facts, we will be unable to think carefully when we need to.

Consider this statement: the divorce revolution—the steady displacement of a marriage culture by a culture of divorce and unwed parenthood—has failed. It has created terrible hardships for children, incurred insupportable social costs, and failed to deliver on its promise of greater adult happiness. The time has come to shift the focus of national attention from divorce to marriage and to rebuild a family culture based on enduring marital relationships.[22] It really is hard to separate the facts from the lies in our culture today. It is hard for us to know who we can believe and who we can trust, especially when we are dealing with a life-changing decision like divorce.

My experience in dealing with either one or both spouses is that they feel life is out of control and now they are ready to change their situation. Like a lot of people, you may feel that it is important to "take control of your life." But what does that mean? Partly, it means being able to properly evaluate the data and claims that bombard you every day with the reality of how things can quickly spin completely out of control. It is important to understand that taking control of your life means knowing you can only control what you can control, and you cannot control others, including your spouse. Therefore, if you cannot distinguish good from faulty reasoning, then you are vulnerable to manipulation and to decisions that are not in your best interest. There are volumes of books and Internet sites full of "facts" about divorce and the effects of divorce. Checking facts is important, because facts are important. We live in a world where facts often take second place to opinion. For many, it depends on what news channel you are watching or news site you read. We must understand that if we behave as though facts don't matter, then one day they won't. Not only can knowing facts change our hearts, but *accepting* them as fact can begin to change the direction we are heading. I

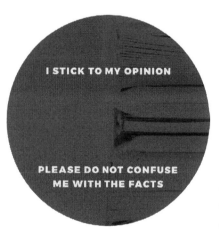

I STICK TO MY OPINION

PLEASE DO NOT CONFUSE ME WITH THE FACTS

am extremely thankful that I have personally witnessed this process in some marriages, and therefore I know it can make a difference. This is one purpose of this book. If self-deception is one of the challenges of keeping a healthy marriage, then it is important to know how these facts will impact you personally. Several people who have gone through a divorce have said to me, "If I only knew then what I know now, then I wouldn't have gone through with my divorce."

We will explore three of divorce's consequences that affect every couple: (1) Financial Consequences, (2) Emotional Consequences, and (3) Family Consequences. It is a common misconception that divorce is a temporary crisis we face only during the time of the divorce process. Some also think that the hurt and pain of divorce will affect only the couple. There is a fallacy that once the acceptable legal arrangements for custody, visits, and child support are made, then the children will soon be fine, and life will go on as normal. This is a misguided understanding of the normal ramifications of divorce. Divorce is a dream that can become a nightmare. I have seen or heard of very few, if any, divorces that go "as planned" with little to no hurt, pain, confusion, custody battles, and financial wars.

Financial Consequences

Public consequences. Divorce has huge public costs. According to a 2003 study, divorce costs the United States $33.3 billion per year. This total includes direct costs to federal and state government for child-support enforcement, Medicaid, Temporary Assistance to Needy Families (TANF), food stamps, and public housing; it also includes indirect costs for correctional facilities, taking care of single elderly people and unwed parents, drug problems, delinquency, and other social problems related to divorce. The average divorce costs state and federal governments $30,000 in direct and indirect costs.[23] The fact is, in a very real way, divorce is very expensive! This is a financial cost that our entire country pays for.

Private consequences. Recognizing the facts about public financial consequences may or may not impact our decision about getting divorced, but looking at how the financial consequences impact us personally is another story. The financial costs to individual divorcing couples are often substantial. Nationwide, the typical fee that each spouse pays a divorce attorney is $250 per hour, and it can be up to as much as $500 per hour plus expenses. Including total attorney's fees, court costs, and other costs, such as hiring a real-estate appraiser, tax advisor, child custody evaluator, or another expert, one survey reported a total cost of around $15,500, including $12,800 in attorney's fees.[24]

There are also many additional costs that usually are not thought about: housing; moving expenses; transportation; potential loss of income during divorce proceedings and transition; additional occupational training; child care, particularly for custodial spouse; partial loss of retirement benefits; and sometimes additional costs to state government, extended family members, and charities if a divorcing parent's initial income is minimal. These financial costs usually continue for years after the divorce papers are served. There may also be considerable financial consequences during retirement for the husband, wife, or both. One report cited that families that were not poor before the divorce see their income drop as much as 50 percent after divorce.[25] This means that some will begin to live below the poverty level for the first time in their life.

Many people believe that the number one reason for marital problems is money, and yet they do not realize that after a divorce it will become a greater problem—not only in the current situation, but in the future as well. It is not uncommon for divorced couples to begin to live below the poverty level as they double most if not all of their expenses.

Emotional Consequences

As impactful as the financial consequences are for the entire family, they do not come close to the impact and damage of the potential emotional consequences, which can last for years, if not the rest of people's lives. I have seen emotional damage in children of all ages. It is not even limited to children who are still living in the home during the divorce; adult children can be impacted just as much. People often view divorce as a way to end the fighting. Unfortunately, the problems, anger, and stress usually don't go away after divorce, but intensify. Often, anger and animosity only increase through the divorce process and for many years to come.

Here are some the common emotions felt during the divorce process. I will not expand on these, as most are self-explanatory, but I just want to make you aware of the emotional toll divorce can take:

- Guilt or shame over having a marriage fail
- Guilt over your own behavior that led to the divorce
- Sadness over losing emotional and financial support
- Depression over losing a home, possessions, and/or income
- Depression related to losing time with your children
- Stress over losing even more than you hope or imagine
- Fear that you will not find another romantic partner
- Fear about having financial struggles following the divorce
- Fear that your children will be negatively impacted
- General anger
- Low self-esteem
- Less satisfaction with your life

Obviously, these emotions can be part of all marriages even before divorce occurs, and they will play a part in even the healthiest of marriages. The important thing to know is these can be addressed if they are recognized before they get out of control. These should be understood as warning signs that you may need to address before there is a breakdown.

I want to highlight two emotions that can appear as result of divorce but are not always considered: grief and suicide. I stated in the introduction that death can be part of the divorce process because "the two become one flesh," and they are being torn apart. It is natural to be sad when your marriage ends. Grieving over the death of your marriage can be a very painful experience, but it is a healthy response. It is important to know the five stages of grief—denial, anger, bargaining, depression, and acceptance— and then to deal with each of these appropriately. The future is uncertain, and therefore so is people's security in who they are and what their purpose is in life. Unfortunately, that in turn can lead to suicide.

Suicide is a real and unfortunate emotional consequence of divorce. A 2000 national study found that divorced men and women are more than twice as likely to commit suicide.[26] The decision to end a relationship can be traumatic, chaotic, and filled with contradictory emotions. There are also specific feelings, attitudes, and dynamics associated with both the initiator and the receiver of the decision to break up. It is not unusual for the initiator to experience fear, relief, distance, impatience, resentment, doubt, and guilt. Likewise, the party who has not initiated the divorce may feel shock, betrayal, loss of control, victimization, decreased self-esteem, insecurity, anger, a desire to get even, and a desire to reconcile. These feelings and emotions are legitimate even if a couple has struggled in their marriage for years; the finality of divorce papers being served can bring out unprecedented emotional pain.

These emotions can drastically affect your decision-making process when it comes to family, finances, and your future. These emotional challenges are not just for the moment but can—and in many cases will—be lifelong. With more than thirty years of research, we now know divorce seldom leads to a better life, as noted in these facts about life after divorce:

- Life expectancies for divorced men and women are significantly lower than for married people (who have the longest life expectancies).
- One study found that those who were unhappy but stayed married were more likely to be happy five years later than those who divorced.
- The health consequences of divorce are so severe that a Yale researcher concluded that "being divorced and a nonsmoker is slightly less dangerous than smoking a pack a day and staying married."
- After a diagnosis of cancer, married people are more likely to recover, while the divorced are less likely to recover, indicating that the emotional trauma of divorce has a long-term impact on the physical health of the body.
- Men and women both suffer a decline in mental health following divorce, but researchers have found that women are more greatly affected. Some of the mental-health indicators impacted by divorce include depression, hostility, self-acceptance, personal growth, and positive relations with others.[27]

The end of a marriage is particularly painful for persons who do not expect or want it. It is even more problematic when this sense of loss is combined with hostile and tense interactions between divorced spouses. Some people who divorce also experience feelings of rejection and embarrassment and may withdraw from their social group. These facts about potential emotional consequences are real no matter who is at fault or who initiates the divorce. These emotions can be devastating, no matter if you are male or female, no matter your economic status or personality type. Emotions are real, and therefore it is important to be prepared to really deal with them.

Family Consequences

As great as both the financial and emotional consequences of divorce can be, the potential long-term damage to family relationships can be even greater and more painful. We're used to hearing ourselves and others say that the most important things in life are family and friends. It's hard to disagree, and the evidence supporting this is overwhelming. If we are honest with ourselves about the facts and nothing but the facts when it comes to both the financial and emotional consequences of divorce, it is obvious that there will be family consequences as well. The obvious damage can be the breakdown of the parent-child relationship, but it is so much more than that. All the in-law relationships, no matter how strong they might be, will at the very least be splintered and awkward. Again, it is important to understand that these consequences are not a momentary inconvenience but will resurface at school activities, sporting events, weddings, and funerals.

The more obvious and well-documented family consequence of divorce is on your immediate family, including your children. As a youth pastor for over twenty years, I have seen this firsthand, and it is one of the big reasons I chose to write this book. I have witnessed the long-term consequences that impact children—including adults—far too many times. I have put my heart and soul into trying to help hundreds of children and teens over the years. Jesus said, "do not hinder children coming to me." I personally have taken this charge very seriously. Children matter to God. Your children matter to Him. All children are a gift from God, and we owe it to them not to hinder them. And yet the facts are overwhelmingly clear in indicating that children and their emotional, social, and spiritual well-being can be drastically impacted by divorce. For some, this affects them for the rest of their lives.

It is not my desire to bog you down with statistics about the effects of divorce on children, but when we understand they are a gift from God and He tells us not to hinder them, then I do think it is important to have a clear understanding of the potential consequences for them. It is obvious that a large number of children of divorced parents survive the experience and later become capable and stable adults. But it is also becoming increasingly evident that many children of divorced parents are at risk of developing detrimental behaviors, personality disorders, and disruptive lifestyles. Each year, over one million American children suffer through their parents' divorce. Half of the children born this year to parents who are married will see their parents divorce before they turn eighteen. Mounting evidence in social-science journals demonstrates that the devastating physical, emotional, and financial effects of divorce on these children will last well into adulthood and affect future generations. Among these broad and damaging effects are the following:

- Children of divorced parents perform more poorly in reading, spelling, and math. They are also more likely to repeat a grade and to have higher dropout rates and lower rates of college graduation.
- Families with children that were not poor before the divorce see their income drop as much as 50 percent. Almost 50 percent of parents who are going through a divorce move into poverty after the divorce.
- Religious worship, which has been linked to better health, longer marriages, and better family life, drops after the parents divorce.
- Children whose parents have divorced are increasingly the victims of abuse. They exhibit more health, behavioral, and emotional problems, are involved more frequently in crime and drug abuse, and have higher rates of suicide.
- A 2004 study found that young women who experience parental divorce are twice as likely to cohabit before marriage and to have a child out of wedlock, when compared to those raised by their married biological parents.[28]

Some research does indicate that the majority of children of divorced parents do not manifest problems that can be outwardly noticed or measured. But the absence of an observably disordered behavior does not mean an absence of emotional distress. A significant number of children of divorce apparently do experience a variety of emotional problems that often go undetected until late adolescence or early and even later adulthood.

Having talked with many children of divorced parents over the years, children of all ages including those in their adult years, there seems to be several common struggles they deal with as they get older and carry into other relationships. These relationships are in all relationships including family, work and friendships. Here is a list some of common struggles that I've heard and observed:

- **Commitment**. Fear of commitment is typical for adult children of divorced parents. Among the most basic and vital things violated by divorce is commitment. Some children deal with that fear of commitment by making a personal decision to avoid marriage.
- **Emotional instability**. For some this a temporary struggle, and yet can also cause emotional scars of fear, abandonment, instability, or insecurity. Some of that is caused by growing up and surrounded by endless bickering and arguing. There are some who marry, but remain emotionally unavailable.
- **Weakened Parent-Child Relationships**. One of the primary effects of divorce (and of the parental conflict that precedes the divorce) is a decline in the relationship between parent and child.
- **Guarded heart**. This can create an unwillingness to be vulnerable or transparent in dealing with your feelings. Some struggle with saying "I love you" with a fear of no longer being loveable.
- **Trust issues**. Children have seen how fast trust can be shredded with their parents. Some see their parents talk about how they trusted each other through marital vows only to walk away from those same vows. They trusted their parents to keep the family together, and experienced how easily broken those trusts were.
- **Being self-conscientious**. Watching the divorce of parents can stir up a feeling of losing all control. It becomes a struggle to try to keep control over yourself and the environment around you. Some children develop low self-esteem due to divorce. They think that they are the cause of divorce and consider their selves worthless.
- **People pleaser or manipulator**. Because children had to go back and forth with parents, some children either show parents as much love and appreciation as they can so they wouldn't feel like they we're favoring one over the other, or try to play each parent off the other through manipulation. For some as they get married are willing to settle for so little from their partner because the fear of rejection is overwhelming. They are willing do anything to try to keep the relationship together.
- **Fear of abandonment**. Some children believe that the people they love will leave them one way or the other. A person who has experienced abandonment is often more likely to encounter long-term psychological challenges. These concerns are typically based primarily on the fear that abandonment will recur. A child who was physically abandoned by a parent or caregiver may struggle with mood swings or anger throughout life, and these behaviors may alienate

potential intimate partners and friends.[29] There can be a tendency to be clingy in relationships because they can't help but imagine the day they'll disappear.

- **Overly affectionate**. Households found that about one in five divorced fathers had not seen his children in the past year, and fewer than half the fathers saw their children more than a few times a year.[30] Children need the affection from their fathers whom they usually only see part-time following a divorce, and therefore they are going to look for it elsewhere. Children and especially daughters may latch on to the first person who gives them attention or may pursue someone who really doesn't want a relationship with them just to fill a void.

The stories that I've heard over the years show how these struggles can carry their parents' divorce into adulthood. It is no wonder that they have a higher risk of divorce themselves. Children of divorce are twice as likely to divorce compared to the offspring of married parents, according to a national longitudinal study of two generations.[31] It is also evident that adults who have experienced parental divorce are less likely to have frequent contact and close relationships with their parents than are adult children from intact families.

Not only do children face consequences through divorce, but when couples divorce, their friendships with others often change or end completely. Those getting the divorce often feel uncomfortable being around couples, as doing so may remind them of what they have lost, or they may be concerned about the level of support they receive from the couples. In turn, couples often feel uncomfortable being around a divorcing person when they have been friends with both spouses. They may fear having to take sides or that their own marital relationship could be threatened when their friends break up.

Often, people do not consider how the divorce will affect extended family. As you separate from your spouse, you may feel some awkwardness from your relatives, causing tension at a time when you are looking for support. Your parents or siblings may have a difficult time talking to you about it or may even be distant because they don't know what to do for you. They may also be unsure of how to feel about the change in the family dynamic, because everyone needs to time to accept it. Again, this can come up years later when you come face to face at school events, weddings, and even funerals.

Making sense of these facts and facts from other studies on the impact of divorce can be overwhelming; however, it is important to regard them as more than just someone's opinion. I strongly encourage you to take time to consider the impact that divorce might have on you, your children, your in-laws, and your friends. It is important to make decisions based upon a balance of emotions, facts, and potential future consequences.

Recounting Real Relationships

(This is a family that I know, but they have requested to remain anonymous)

My journey started when I was in my second year of college. My boyfriend of four years and I found out that we were pregnant. The news of the pregnancy led us quickly to the altar. Our dating relationship had been a rocky one, and that continued throughout our marriage. I dropped out of college to raise my child, and my husband graduated with a teaching degree. My husband was offered a teaching position, along with a coaching position. By this time, I had two young children and a baby on the way. The coaching position involved many long hours away from home, as well as many nights hanging out in local bars with the other coaches. Unfortunately, the bar life directly resulted in infidelity in our marriage. We managed to stay together for many years after the infidelity, but we struggled, to say the least.

When our youngest child went to college, I moved out of my home and filed for divorce. I thought the divorce would bring me happiness and peace. However, this was the beginning of the most hurtful and darkest times in my life. The divorce went quietly and without a lot of arguing, but the ripple effect of my divorce was yet to be seen. I do believe the Lord was speaking to me and showing me I should go back to my marriage during this time, but I was so sick of all the issues in my marriage, I didn't listen. My heart was broken, my family was broken, and I was an emotional mess. This was actually the first and only time I contemplated taking my own life. The Lord faithfully carried me out of the depression I was going through.

Within two years of my divorce, I was remarried to a gentleman I met at church. Once again, the Lord was speaking to me not to marry, but I felt so much pressure from my new husband and from other family members that I thought I would look bad if I cancelled the wedding, so I proceeded with it. To anyone who is reading this right now and considering getting remarried, I beg you to step back and really pray on this. Do not make major, life-changing decisions unless you are in a good place emotionally.

I found myself trying to focus on this new marriage. I was also trying to be there for my kids, my kids were trying to figure out where they fit in, and I was trying to figure out where I fit in with my new husband and his kids. Everything about it felt awkward and so uncomfortable for everyone concerned. Because of other extended-family issues that became time-consuming, my head was spinning. I honestly didn't know what was up or down. Everywhere I turned there was an issue. The only thing I knew was to PRAY.

I slowly watched all of our children fall apart. One of our children went through four years of alcohol abuse, another became angry with me and our relationship became estranged, and yet another child was involved in an unhealthy relationship. My husband's child was headed for prison for a drunk-driving incident that took the lives of her two friends, and both my husband's sons were battling drug and alcohol abuse. I honestly believe that all these issues were the direct result of a broken, hurting family whose solid foundation was shaken. The battle before us seemed insurmountable. But by God's grace and our strong faith, one by one our children were being delivered out of the enemies' hands. God is so faithful!

These are the things I wish I had focused more on before considering divorce:

1) Get spiritually healthy and emotionally healthy before you make any life decision.
2) Focus on God, not on your spouse. Seek Him, listen to Him, no matter what your feelings are telling you or what other people are telling you.
3) Pray, pray, pray.
4) Seek out a trusted couple who will pray for you, come alongside you, and encourage you to stay in your marriage.
5) Do not make any major decisions when you are not in a good place emotionally.
6) Put God and your children first and foremost.

God honors the marriage covenant, and God's heart is for family. We need to fight for our marriages. Our children depend on us. It's not about us. It's about honoring God and our families. My marriage now is a good, solid marriage, but my family is *forever* broken. My prayer for all those who are reading this is that you stay close to Jesus, look only to Him. Don't listen to the world. If you do this, I truly believe the Lord will restore your marriage and bless your children. God's blessings over you and your families.

Journey Together
Marriage Workbook

1) Be honest with yourself...how much are you really open to facts verses feelings?

_____

_____

2) As you look into the future and consider the impact of your decision to work on your marriage or get a divorce, how can the facts listed in this chapter play a greater role?

_____

_____

_____

3) As you look back at all the statistics and facts presented in this chapter; list the things that stand out the most in each of these categories:

Financial Consequences – Emotional Consequences – Family Consequences

_____	_____	_____
_____	_____	_____
_____	_____	_____

4) Allow that list to connect the eighteen inches from your head to your heart. Write down what you see as your potential future concerning these facts.

_____

_____

_____

5) Solomon, the wisest man who ever lived, said, "Children are a gift from the LORD; they are a reward from him" (Psalms 127:3, NLT). What does that mean to you as you think about your own children? How might that impact the steps you take next?

_____

6) What is your reaction to the items in the list "Ten Struggles Children of Divorce Bring into Their Twenties"? Are there one or two points that affect you more than the others?

_____

_____

_____

7) Look back at the list of some of the common emotions felt during the divorce process. Are there three or four in that list that you could see as being a potential problem for you?

_____

_____

_____

8) Discuss how divorce can be like dealing with a death in the family.

_____

_____

_____

9) Look back to the research about life after divorce. Do any of these facts stand out as a surprise? Are any of them a concern for you?

_____

_____

_____

10) Look back over the list "Ten Struggles Children of Divorce Bring into Their Twenties." Have you seen any of these in friends or family members? Do any of the items trouble you as you think about your own children?

_____

_____

_____

PRAY

Here is a prayer to get you started, and remember: it's not the words that matter so much as what's in your heart. Read it out loud:

Dear Heavenly Father, I know that You want me to face the truth and that I must be honest with You. I know that choosing to believe the truth will set me free. I realize that there are times I have been deceived by Satan, the father of lies, and I have deceived myself as well. I ask you to open my eyes to You and the truth of what my decision will do for me, my spouse, my children, and the future of all of us.

I ask You, Father, to look deep inside me and know my heart. Show me if there is anything in me that I am trying to hide, because I want to be open and honest with you and with myself. In Jesus's Name, Amen.

CHAPTER 3
Fiction Disguised as Truth

"It is wise to direct your anger toward problems—not people;
to focus your energies on answers—not excuses."
WILLIAM ARTHUR WARD

An elementary-school teacher gave each child in her class the first half of a well-known proverb and asked them to come up with the remainder of the proverb. These are the results:

- Better to be safe than…punch a fifth-grader. (Proverb: Better to be safe than sorry.)
- A rolling stone…plays the guitar. (Proverb: A rolling stone gathers no moss.)
- The squeaking wheel gets…annoying. (Proverb: The squeaking wheel gets the grease.)
- I think, therefore I…get a headache. (Proverb: I think, therefore I am.)
- There is nothing new under the…bed. (Proverb: There is nothing new under the sun.)
- A penny saved is…not much. (Proverb: A penny saved is a penny earned.)
- The grass is always greener…when you leave the sprinkler on. Or, the grass is always greener…when you put manure on it. (Proverb: The grass is always greener on the other side of the fence.)

Truth In Fiction

Personally, I have never been a big fan of reading fiction, although I remember reading three works of fiction, and I did really enjoy each of them. All three books highlighted truth in a way that was very engaging. They gave me spiritual insights that were tremendously powerful. Two of the books, *This Present Darkness* and *Piercing the Darkness*, were written by Frank E. Peretti and emphasized the power of prayer. The other book just came out as a movie this year, *The Shack*, by William P. Young. It is important to know that there may be some truth in these stories, but they are fiction; they are just stories.

Stephen King, an American author of horror stories, supernatural fiction, suspense, and science fiction says, "Fiction is the truth inside the lie." In Hollywood, marriage has been depicted through fiction, fabrication, and fantasies so much that it is hard to know what to believe. Galadriel in *The Lord of the Rings* says, "And some things that should not have been forgotten were lost. History became legend. Legend became myth. And for two and a half thousand years, the ring passed out of all knowledge."

Think about that: history becomes legend and legend becomes myth. As long as humans have told each other stories, truths have been transformed into legends and eventually myths. Consequently, fiction and myths can become powerful weapons of mass deception.

One such myth that expresses some people's view and inner reality is: "The grass is always greener on the other side of the fence." The acceptance of this misconception or lie can create a lot of damage, especially when it comes to marriage. Think about how it can be wrongly applied in relationships:

- People who are single are sure they would be happier if they were married.
- Married people feel convinced they would be happier if they were to get divorced.
- Divorced people feel they would be happier if they had never been married at all.

We need to understand how vicious, debilitating, imprisoning, and deceptive the "grass is always greener on the other side" mentality is. Often it is because you buy into the deception that the grass is greener on the other side that you never began to look at your own lawn. You see other people's success and begin to reason with yourself why they deserve it, but you don't. You see other people's success in their life, their career or marriage and you begin to question why their situations are so much better than yours. The truth is "The grass is greener where you water it and take care of it."

While many of have fallen prey to this trap it is important that you refuse to go there or remain there if that's where you already are at. Many believe comparing yourself or your marriage to others actually helps you on to move forward faster, but most of the time it only leaves you discouraged, disillusioned, and dejected. Figuratively, if we were willing to water it and tend to it, we then could watch it grow and thrive. Healthy marriages don't happen through neglect. It takes time to invest in a healthy marriage, effort to create intimacy, and consistency to connect with your spouse. No matter how "healthy" or "unhealthy" your marriage is, it is essential to constantly put time, effort, and love into it and to make it a priority. So, before you diagnose your marriage with a fatal case of failure to thrive, feed it, nurture it, and give your marriage at least as much attention as you would give to your escape plans.

As with everything that is important to us in life, your intentions drive your attentions. It is important to identify myths, fictional stories, or lies that can lead to a broken relationship. When you allow truth to be hindered by thoughts that fester and penetrate your heart, your thoughts could spiral out of control and then set your marriage up for failure. If that happens, then you might begin to pull away from your spouse emotionally and/or physically, without even recognizing you are doing so. It is through this deception that your heart can grow cold, and you become oblivious to the truth. So, before you

| YOUR INTENTIONS DRIVE YOUR ATTENTIONS |

call it quits, make *staying* your focus and your intention. Obviously, attention alone will not guarantee greener grass, but at least be intentional before you look over the fence and begin to climb it.

We do owe it to our spouse, our children, and our future to at least try to nurture the marriage before making a decision. The grass isn't greener on the other side; it's greener where you water it. Pick up the hose and water, and fertilize your marriage until you see green grass again. The reason the "grass is greener" myth is so detrimental to our marriage and our mental health is that it can turn us away from the basic life principle of making the most of what we have. In an age and time of entitlement, it is vital for you to recognize just how blessed you really are.

Marriage Fiction or Real Truth

We might think that lies can no longer be disguised as truth in this age of technology where information is available at our fingertips, but we are proven wrong time and again. More information does not lead to greater critical thinking. When a lie is repeated often enough, it becomes truth—or rather, it appears true. Here are several statements that have been repeated in so many divorce stories that they have become accepted as real truth:

THE KEY TO SUCCEEDING IN MARRIAGE IS NOT FINDING THE RIGHT PERSON; IT'S LEARNING TO LOVE THE PERSON YOU FOUND.

Fiction: "I married the wrong person."

For the sake of argument, let's pretend you did marry the "wrong" person. If so, you are not alone, because in hindsight it's easy to play Monday-morning quarterback and look back at what you should or could have done differently. Even if you wish the circumstances or timing had been different, that doesn't change where you are right now. Movie star Mickey Rooney said, "Marriage is like batting in baseball; when the right one comes along, you don't want to let it go by." It sounds good until you realize that Mickey himself was married eight times. He must have had a lot of "good pitches" to swing at! According to this viewpoint, there's only one spouse, or that one "soul mate," with whom you could be happy. The lie is that you need to find that "right" person, even if it means discarding a spouse who no longer "works" for you. Even if you believe you made a mistake when you married, you cannot fix it by divorcing. Two wrongs do not make a right.

Real Truth:

When the two of you walked down the aisle, each of you became the right person for the other. The success of a marriage has little to do with marrying the wrong or the right person. According to author and speaker Mark Gungor,

> The truth is, a successful marriage is not the result of marrying the *right* person, feeling the *right* emotions, thinking the *right* thoughts, or even praying the *right* prayers. It's about doing the *right* thing—period. You may look back and second-guess your reasons, but you entered into a covenant in which learning to truly love someone takes a lifetime.[32]

Is your spouse perfect? No, but neither are you. Welcome to the human race. We've all made bad choices in life relating to finances, career, and health. We've made bad choices by gossiping and lying. And yes, we've made bad choices in relationships. This list of bad choices can go on and on for all of us, and we shouldn't just walk away from them. We need to learn and grow from them. We need to learn to make adjustments to make sure we don't do the same thing again. We might suffer terribly because of our choices, or maybe because of the choices others make that affect us, but we must know that God can create unforeseen blessings out of them.

If you believe the lie that you didn't marry the right person, then you must know that the key to succeeding in marriage is not finding the right person; it's learning to love the person you found. God's principles of love, acceptance, patience, and forgiveness work not only in our own life, but through us to pass on that same love, acceptance, patience, and forgiveness to others. God's love and forgiveness works all the time, every time—no matter to whom you are married.

Fiction: "It would be easier to start over with someone new than to try and fix our relationship."

Life is not easy. It will be hard, and hard times are going to come your way. Grief, pain, anger, disappointment, hurt, tears—you'll face them all in this lifetime. I wish I could promise you otherwise, but unfortunately I have lived a life that bears out that truth. You will face the death of people you love, you will find yourself lost in the gulf of hurt and pain, you will be betrayed by those closest to you, and you will go through periods of devastating self-doubt.

"LIFE IS HARD; IT'S HARDER IF YOU'RE STUPID."

- JOHN WAYNE

It is not about life being easier, but knowing what will it cost you. Starting over doesn't mean that you won't be taking all the unresolved pain and conflict with you into a new relationship. You will eventually have to deal with it either way. Knowing the cost and pain of divorce, it is important to recognizing that you will most likely be better off fixing what you have rather than throwing it away. You may have a lot more to lose if you start over with a lot of unknowns than if you set out to fix what you know to be true. When you've been through lots of difficulties and frustrations in your marriage, it may seem easier to pull the ejection lever and imagine starting over with somebody new, but it should be noted that second marriages have a much higher rate of divorce than first marriages. It really is important to ask why that is! You can start over with the person you are with right now. Because of who God is, you can begin to fix the relationship you are in right now.

Real Truth:

Struggles in life arise for a reason, and they can be helpful in providing experience or a lesson. Life is hard, and tough times are certain. But how you comport yourself during those times defines who you really are and will define your future. God didn't create marriage to make life easy. God created marriage to reveal beauty, depth, strength, and love that could never be discovered in a land of "easy." It is not easier to start over with someone new, because problems and emotions are not solved by a second marriage. The problems are still there, only now you have to deal with attorneys, judges, visitation complications, parenting differences—all while still having to solve the same old problems that were part of the first marriage. Working on and then fixing your marriage can seem like an overwhelming task, but if you step aside from the issues at hand, rekindling your marriage is an accomplishable goal.

God is into bringing dead people back to life. If you consider your marriage as dead, it is well within His ability to bring you and your spouse a new love, a new hope, a new beginning...if you are willing. A very good place to start is to say with conviction that divorce is off the table and decide that you want to fix your marriage. This was a decision my wife and I made very early in our marriage. We never made divorce an option or threat. I can remember many conversations over the years with children who feared their parents would divorce because they mentioned it during arguments in front of their children. Fear of the possibility of divorce is obviously not as bad as divorce itself, but for children it can be devastating even to think about it.

Fiction: "I've fallen out of love," or "I love you, but I'm just not *in* love with you."

Chapter 4 will explore this topic of love and feelings, but for now it is important to know that we cannot "fall in love" any more than we can "fall out of love." To fall is something involuntary, outside of our control, not necessarily unwished for, but hardly something we can plan. Choice is the essential element of love. Pure and simple love does not simply appear or disappear. The feeling that you are "falling out of love" is an important warning sign letting you know something is interfering with your connection with your spouse.

Real Truth:

Love is a choice that is made evident through our actions. True love is enduring, and only in marriage does it come with a lifelong commitment to another person. Love is satisfying in so many ways, but all too often people associate love with things that really don't have anything to do with love. Many marriages have been transformed when people discovered they can and need to *choose* to love. If your concept of love has anything to do with falling into or out of love, then you will miss what actually love is, because love is, thankfully, so much more. We know from God's word that love is a verb to show that an action is taking place. Love is an action. A quick look at 1 Corinthians 13:4–8, which is a passage read in a lot of wedding ceremonies, describes true love. You will see that not one word or verse describes falling into or out of love. The good news is that once you choose to practice the Bible's love principles, you also begin to experience emotional love. Love is a choice you can make every day regardless of how your spouse responds or what he or she does. "Love never fails" (1 Corinthians 13:8).

> Love is patient, love is kind. It does not envy, it does not boast, it is not proud. It is not rude, it is not self-seeking, it is not easily angered, it keeps no record of wrongs. Love does not delight in evil but rejoices with the truth. It always protects, always trusts, always hopes, always perseveres. Love never fails. (1 Corinthians 13:4-8)

Fiction: "I'm so unhappy. This can't be what God wants, because He wants me to be happy."

Many people divorce because they are unhappy. It may be true that you're unhappy, but it's a lie to think that your spouse has the power or the responsibility to make you happy. Putting pressure on your spouse to create your happiness places an unrealistic burden on both of you and puts more value on your inconsistent feelings than on your unwavering commitment. If you believe that God doesn't want you to be miserable, you're right. However, He wants you to find happiness and seek relief His way. The Psalmist says, "This is the day the Lord has made; let us rejoice and be glad in it" (Psalms 118:24). If we think we can find happiness when we disobey God and take things into our own hands, then we really are deceiving ourselves and will pay a huge price. When we disobey God, we turn away from the source of joy, which comes from following Jesus Christ.

Real Truth:

God's desire for us to be happy doesn't mean there won't be times when we're not. We will go through seasons of suffering and difficulty—that's life. The truth is, God's desire for us is more than happiness. Author and international speaker Gary Thomas says, "Marriage is not meant to make you happy, rather, holy. Marriage is sanctifying. God can and will use this trial and tribulation in your marriage for his glory and your sanctification."[33] The Apostle Paul clearly states that the main purpose of marriage "is to make her holy…without stain or wrinkle or any other blemish, but holy and blameless" (Ephesians 5:26–27).

God wants to refine our character, help us heal from the past, and develop our spiritual potential to help us become more like Him. This process can feel painful and not very pleasant. There is nothing wrong with wanting happiness, because God wants it for us too. It's just a matter of not exalting it over God and His work in our life. It's an issue of being willing to surrender to Him for those seasons when we don't feel so happy, while trusting that His blessings are still on the way. Happiness is circumstantial. Joy is superior and supernatural. Biblical joy gains assurance even in the midst of trials and has nothing to do with the circumstances we are going through. When you stop concentrating on how unhappy you are, you will find that your happiness is growing.

Fiction: "We just grew apart."

Couples do grow apart, but it doesn't "just" happen. It is a choice, innocent or not. But just as "falling out of love" is a lie, so is "we just grew apart." Things don't just happen. Growth is a process, not an event. If there is going to be growth, then you have to be intentional in the process. You may think you and your spouse have incompatible personalities. Or you may not share similar beliefs, values, or interests. Perhaps your sex life is unsatisfying. Whatever the frustration, the answer is to learn how to flourish in your situation while working to improve it, not run away. One of the most common issues with couples who are struggling in marriage is a lack of intentional investment in their marriage.

Real Truth:

Making an intentional choice to work at something can prevent growing apart from happening. Take action now to grow together to make sure that growing apart never "just" happens. Marriage can be extremely messy. As we "all have sinned and fallen short" of being perfect, then we can do dumb things in marriage—we hurt one another, we make false assumptions and then miscommunicate, we manipulate or say unkind things to our spouse, and we think less about serving the other and more about being served. Growth is a process that must be intentional. If you are serious about your marriage, then the driving force must be pursuing a living, loving relationship with your spouse and with Christ that will deepen as you get to know Him better. That was Paul's prayer: "And we pray this in order that you may live a life worthy of the Lord and may please him in every way: bearing fruit in every good work, growing in the knowledge of God" (Colossians 1:10).

Fiction: "We serve a forgiving God. He will forgive me," or "We live under grace. Don't be legalistic."

It is true that God forgives us. It is true God has always been full of grace: "Let your remorse tear at your hearts and not your garments. Return to the Lord your God, for he is gracious and merciful. He is not easily angered; he is full of kindness and anxious not to punish you" (Joel 2:13, TLB).

There is no conflict between grace and obeying God when it is properly understood. Christ fulfilled the Law on our behalf and offers the power of the Holy Spirit, who motivates a regenerated heart to live in obedience to Him. Biblical grace has the power to save as well as the power to motivate a sinful heart toward godliness. When we do not have a desire to be godly, then we do not know God's grace through faith in Christ. It is important to know about God's forgiveness and grace, but it is vital to trust and receive God's forgiveness and grace through a life in Christ. We will explore this further in Chapter 6.

Real Truth:

Grace is God's nature and the nature of all who love Him. It is expressed through things like forgiveness, kindness, mercy, and gentleness. God's Word never encourages us to sin, while at the same time it speaks of God's forgiveness. You can count on His forgiveness when you genuinely confess your sin, but not when you harden your heart and disobey Him. The Apostle Paul writes: "What shall we say, then? Shall we go on sinning so that grace may increase? By no means! We died to sin; how can we live in it any longer?" (Romans 6:1–2, NCV). Grace is forgiveness without consequences. For example, a man commits adultery against his wife. The wife forgives, but he still needs to be accountable for his actions until trust is rebuilt. If his wife gives grace,

FORGIVENESS IS OUR RESPONSE TO GOD'S GRACE

it is as if there was no offense at all, and she offers her trust. When we see God's grace for what it is, we will be driven to our knees in confession of sin. Once we've been completely honest, broken, and repentant, we'll experience that amazing grace. When we experience His amazing grace, we have the capacity to forgive beyond anything we can imagine.

Fiction: "The kids will be fine."

Even if you are a rational separating couple making every effort not to fight in front of your children, make no mistake—they know what is going on. It's true that our kids *may* be fine, but are we willing to take that risk? Hopefully you have taken an honest look at the facts about children of divorce in the previous chapter. If you have children, no matter their age, they will be impacted by divorce. When children are older, we may think they can handle going through the process of divorce because they have lived in dysfunction for so long, but divorce is a deliberate decision to destroy the most important relationship parents provide to the child: a family. In many ways, children can be negatively affected in greater ways than you can ever imagine. The divorce of a child's parents, even if those children are nearly grown or adults themselves, almost always has emotionally devastating consequences. To believe otherwise is to believe one of the most dangerous lies about divorce.

Real Truth:

"Children are a gift from the Lord. Don't make your children bitter about life. Instead, bring them up in Christian discipline and instruction" (Psalms 127:3; Ephesians 6:4, GW).

Your divorce will impact your children. Since 1974, about one million children per year have seen their parents divorce—and children who are exposed to divorce are two to three times more likely than their peers whose parents' marriage is intact to suffer from serious social or psychological pathologies, as discussed in chapter 2.

Fiction: "We'll never be able to make it work."

Your marriage may look hopeless right now, but it can still work if you are willing to work. It may not be easy, but it can not only work, it can be better than you ever dreamed of before you said "I do." Couples can and have come back from terrible places in their relationship to create amazing marriages. Couples who make it are not the ones who never had a reason to get divorced, they're the ones who decide that their commitment to one another is always more important than their differences and flaws. Keep fighting for each other, and don't give up! Your marriage is always worth the effort.

Real Truth:

We see in the Bible that a young boy's father brings his sick son to Jesus and asks Him if can heal his son. "If you can?" said Jesus. "Everything is possible for him who believes" (Mark 9:23). Never say never, especially if you are doing what God says is best for you and your family. Never say you can never do something, because that is closing the door to the possibility that it *could* be done! Your marriage can work… if you are willing. Achieving success in life, work, and relationships requires an understanding of how to stop making excuses. Excuses are often made to shift blame to circumstances beyond our control. If you hear yourself saying that you cannot stay married because of something your spouse has done, is doing, or is not doing, then you are shifting the blame to someone or something outside of yourself. Ultimately, what you do is your responsibility, and remember: the grass is greener where you water it, take care of it, and fertilize it. The final three chapters of this book will give some insights into how you can make your marriage work.

Recounting Real Relationships

(This is a family that I know, but they have requested to remain anonymous)

Here is the condensed version of our journey through marriage, divorce, and the rebuilding of our family. My husband and I met when he got out of the army. We married when we were in our early twenties. We had our first son three years later. My mother died suddenly from a heart attack that year. I remember saying, "I will never love that much again, because it hurts too much to lose them!" Neither of us realized the impact that statement would immediately have on our lives and our marriage. I shut down my emotions, except for the anger...anger at God for taking my mom and anger at my husband because I didn't feel he was being emotionally supportive. He felt emotionally abandoned by me too, because I closed myself off from him. He also used anger to cope with life, having lived in an abusive and alcoholic home where he was emotionally and physically abandoned.

We both used alcohol to deaden the pain we were feeling. As the relationship deteriorated, so did our finances, caring for our boys, and our family environment. The increasing alcohol use in our home only added more pain to a very dysfunctional situation. We started looking outside the relationship to have our needs met, which also increased the breakdown of the marriage. The problem is, when you have two people in a household with that much pain, handling our daily responsibilities, let alone being there for our sons, was nearly impossible. The only solution we could see to this situation was to end our thirteen-year marriage.

Even with a tremendous amount of dysfunction in our home, there were good times throughout those years: we had our second son, built our careers, and developed a strong friendship with each other. Amazingly, we still liked each other, but we didn't feel there was any love left in the relationship. We were separated/divorced for three years. During that time we both started our journeys toward recovery from substance abuse and went through many hours of one-on-one counseling. While we were walking the path of recovery and discovering who we were as individuals, the friendship we had built grew even stronger. We started to rebuild the trust, and that was when we realized we still had strong feelings for each other. We dated for a while and ended up getting remarried!

During the next several years we kept working our recovery programs, and we continued counseling. We had recommitted ourselves to the relationship and each other. We have been remarried for twenty-seven years, and we still make a conscious effort to keep improving our communication and growing our relationship. As we reflect back, we can see how God was directing our paths back to Him through this entire journey. We always attended church regularly, and we "knew of" God, but we did not "know" God.

It wasn't until we started attending a church where they talked about having a personal and intimate relationship with Jesus that we started to change ourselves from the inside. We could not have done any of this without God giving us His strength and His mercy to heal our hearts and all the brokenness in our lives. God has been so faithful and merciful throughout our lives! We try to live by the verse from Luke 7:47, "Therefore, I tell you, her many sins have been forgiven—for she loved much. But he who has been forgiven little loves little." We both feel we have been forgiven much, and because of that forgiveness we try to give back and help people heal from their brokenness.

Journey Together
Marriage Workbook

1) Do you like fiction books or movies? If so, why? (Men, before you say you do not like fiction, realize that *Back to the Future* and *Men in Black*, among others, are fiction.)

_____

_____

2) Think about and discuss John Maxwell's quote as stated in this chapter:

I've realized that it is often because you buy into the deception that the grass is greener on the other side that you never began to look at your own lawn. You see other people's success and begin to reason with yourself why they deserve it, but you don't. You see other people's forward progress and console yourself with how much more gifted they are or how better their situations are than yours.

How can comparing ourselves with others and what they have hinder our marriage?

_____

_____

_____

3) If you understand that the grass isn't greener on the other side and it's greener where you water it, then how can you begin to water your relationship so it can grow?

_____

_____

_____

4) Discuss what you can learn from this quote from Mark Gungor as stated in this chapter:

The truth is, a successful marriage is not the result of marrying the *right* person, feeling the *right* emotions, thinking the *right* thoughts, or even praying the *right* prayers. It's about doing the *right* thing—period. You may look back and second-guess your reasons, but you entered into a covenant in which learning to truly love someone takes a lifetime.

_____

_____

_____

5) "Life is hard; it's harder if you're stupid." What do you think this quote, attributed to John Wayne, has to do with decisions we make in regards to our marriage?

_____

_____

_____

6) Why do you think some people believe that you can fall out of love? How can that be justified, knowing that love is a choice that we make and is evident through our actions? What are some elements of love as listed in 1 Corinthians 13:4-8 that can be developed in your relationship?

_____

_____

_____

7) It is important to understand grace. Christ fulfilled the Law on our behalf and offers the power of the Holy Spirit, who motivates a regenerated heart to live in obedience to Him. Read the following verses: Matthew 3:8, Acts 1:8, 1 Thessalonians 1:5, 2 Timothy 1:14, James 2:26. God gives a grace that has the power to save, but it also has the power to motivate a sinful heart toward godliness.

_____

_____

_____

8) Jesus said, "Everything is possible for him who believes" (Mark 9:23). How does it feel to know with God everything is possible, including breathing life and love into your marriage?

_____

_____

_____

PRAY

Here is a prayer to get you started, and remember: it's not the words that matter so much as what's in your heart. Read it out loud:

Lord, I confess that I have deceived myself, comparing myself and our marriage to others. I ask you to help me to nurture and grow my love for my spouse. I thank You for Your forgiveness, and I commit myself to believing Your truth. I believe our marriage is possible, because everything is possible with You. In Jesus's Name, Amen.

CHAPTER 4

Feelings Do Matter

"When we trust God more than our feelings, it confuses the devil. I mean,
when he throws you his best shot and he can't budge you from believing God,
he won't know what to do with you anymore."

JOYCE MEYER

ate one summer evening in Broken Bow, Nebraska, a weary truck driver pulled his rig into an all-night truck stop. The waitress had just served him dinner when three tough-looking, leather-jacketed motorcyclists—Hell's Angels types—decided to give him a hard time. Not only did they verbally abuse him, one grabbed the hamburger off his plate, another took a handful of his french fries, and the third picked up his coffee and began to drink it.

The truck driver calmly got up, picked up his check, walked to the front of the room, put the check and his money on the cash register, and went out the door.

One of the bikers said, "Ain't much of a man, is he?"

The waitress replied, "And he's not much of a truck driver, either. He just ran over three motorcycles on his way out of the parking lot."

No matter what your personality or temperament may be, feelings and emotions will impact your relationships. One thing is certain about feelings: we all have them. Whether it is because of hardships in life or because of our temperament, some people show their emotions more than others, but we all have them. Unfortunately, though, there are times when the emotions have us. It is when the emotions have us that they become a problem.

Understanding your feelings and then dealing with them in the context of marriage can and will drastically impact your relationship, communication, heart, and your love toward each other. Having control over your emotions is not to say that you cannot have feelings. It is, however, important to know how to handle feelings in the best way. Are you in control of your emotions, or are your emotions controlling your relationships and your decisions?

Feelings Are Legitimate: Deal with Them

Feelings and emotions are huge when it comes to relationships, especially when people are dealing with marital conflict and emotions can be extremely high. When emotions are running high, it usually means feelings are very sensitive at that exact moment and can be a little unstable. Feelings are a legitimate and important part of life. We all have them, and the Bible speaks a lot about emotions, both positive and negative: love, joy, peace, patience, anger, bitterness, and hatred. In His human nature, even Jesus showed emotions: weeping when he heard his friend Lazarus had died (John 11), being angry at the way the temple was being used (Mark 11), and showing compassion (Mark 8). The Bible has a positive view on handling our emotions and indicates they are not something to be ignored. Paul says, "Don't sin by letting anger control you. Don't let the sun go down while you are still angry" (Ephesians 4:26, NLT). Our feelings will be on display when we allow anger to destroy our relationship day after day, week after week, and year after year through the root of bitterness. The writer of Hebrews points out that bitterness grows in us and can affect others: "Look after each other so that none of you fails to receive the grace of God. Watch out that no poisonous root of bitterness grows up to trouble you, corrupting many" (Hebrews 12:15, NLT).

In the book of Song of Songs we see a story about a groom and his bride in which feelings are on display in a way that many couples face in regard to love, hurt, forgiveness, and even adultery. We know that some people can wear their emotions on their sleeves and therefore drastically impact what they feel inside and express outwardly, sometimes without a filter. Feelings are so legitimate that they can have a big effect on your physical health as well. When you are angry, stressed, and anxious, your immune system is weakened, and you are at risk for many physical conditions. One of the greatest problems with relying on and making decisions based on our feelings—especially regarding the success of a romantic relationship—is that feelings change, usually daily.

Feelings Are Legitimate: Love Ignites

The Righteous Brothers' 1964 song "You've Lost that Lovin' Feeling" reflects an understanding in our society that love is just a feeling. According to *Wikipedia*, the Righteous Brothers' original version was a critical and commercial success upon its release, becoming a number-one hit single in February 1965 in both the United States and the United Kingdom. It was the fifth best-selling song of 1965 in the United States. In December 1999, the performing-rights organization Broadcast Music, Inc. ranked the song as the most played song on American radio and television in the twentieth century, having accumulated more than eight million airplays by 1999 and nearly fifteen million by 2011. In 2015, the single was inducted into the National Recording Registry by the Library of Congress for being culturally, historically, or aesthetically significant.

Fifty years later, "You've Lost that Lovin' Feeling" is culturally significant because it speaks volumes about our culture's understanding or misunderstanding of what love really is. We should recognize and affirm that love is an emotion. Affections are part of the essence of love. These emotions might not always be intense, but they are always there to some extent. We must also recognize that love is so much more than a just a "loving feeling"; it is indeed an act of the will.

One piece of evidence for this is found in 1 Corinthians 13:1–3, which has by far been one of the most used verses for weddings that I've attended and officiated. This is where Paul says that you can give away all your possessions to the poor and still not have love. Evidently, then, love is more than an act of the will, because you can have a sacrificial act of the will without having love. As you continue to read in verses 4–7 of 1 Corinthians, love is said to involve various actions: "Love is patient and kind; love does not envy or boast; it is not arrogant or rude. It does not insist on its own way; it is not irritable or resentful; it does not rejoice at wrongdoing, but rejoices with the truth. Love bears all things, believes all things, hopes all things, endures all things." All of these characteristics of love mentioned by the Apostle Paul are directed toward the well-being of someone else. That's why love is more than just a powerful feeling. These qualities of love that Paul lists require more than a warm feeling or infatuation. Think about how warm you have to feel to be kind, or be patient, or forgive someone. The love that God says will make a difference in our relationships does not refer to emotion alone, but to an attitude and action, all of which we are able to control. This is a love that is evident and activated in what we say to and do for others. Biblical love is not only a choice to show our will through our actions, but it includes our emotions and affections, all of which will be lived out through every conflict, every difficultly, and every disagreement.

One study reported that the major reasons marriages fail include, in order:

(1)   infidelity
(2)   no longer in love
(3)   emotional problems
(4)   financial problems
(5)   sexual problems
(6)   problems with in-laws
(7)   neglect of children
(8)   physical abuse
(9)   alcohol
(10)   job conflicts
(11)   communication problems
(12)   married too young[34]

Don't miss the order of these reasons. Notice that "physical abuse" was ranked as number eight in reasons for divorce, and "no longer in love" ranked as number two. Way too many marriages seem to end from burnout rather than blowout. Studies reveal that a significant number of these couples could work through their problems, revive their love, and stay married if they actively worked to love their spouse through actions and didn't determine their future based on their feelings. It is important to understand that even if people care deeply for their spouse, this doesn't mean they will always be in touch with positive feelings. They will often have negative feelings, such as doubt, irritation, hurt, and anger. When these feelings begin to dominate our thinking, that's when we can begin to *feel* that we are falling out of love.

LOVE IS A VERB

WITHOUT ACTION IT IS MERELY A WORD

There is a story about a couple whose marriage seemed to get worse with each passing day. The wife finally saw a lawyer and said she wanted a divorce. But she told the lawyer that since her husband had hurt her so many times, she wanted to really put it to him and make him hurt badly before she divorced him. The lawyer told her to go home and start pretending as if she loved him through her actions. He told her to do things for him as if she were totally in love with him. The lawyer said if she did this for three months, her husband would let down his guard, and then she could spring the divorce on him and he would be devastated.

So the woman took his advice, and for three months she did everything she could to convince her husband that she loved him. Three months later, the attorney called and asked if she still wanted the divorce. She said that she didn't, because she had fallen madly in love with her husband all over again.

Take the first step to love your spouse so much it hurts. Emotions cannot be the primary thing that drives us, or drives our marriage relationship. Love is ignited with actions. When you express kindness through a thoughtful act, a kind word, or a gift, you do not have to claim any warm emotional feelings. You simply are being kind. It is in an act of expressing love that you are most likely to receive love from your spouse, which in turn affects your feelings in a positive manner.

Marriage counselor and author Gary Chapman states that the "in love" or infatuation phase, which he believes usually lasts several months to two years, includes the illusion that your partner is perfect in every aspect that matters.[35]

In his book *The Meaning of Marriage*, Timothy Keller says,

We never know whom we marry, we just think we do. Or even if we first marry the right person, just give it a while and he or she will change. For marriage that means we are not the same person after we have entered it. The primary problem is...learning how to love and care for the stranger to whom you find yourself married."[36]

Love, biblical love, can ignite a marriage when we learn and begin to love and care for that person (or stranger) you find yourself married to. Timothy Keller's chapter on "Loving the Stranger" is itself worth the purchase price of the book. I want to highlight a segment of it that clearly explains where many couples are and how living out love God's way will change how you think, reason, and feel about the other person. He first asks, "How do we love each other so that our marriage goes on from strength to strength rather than stalling out in repetitive arguments that end in fruitless silence? The basic answer is that you must speak truth in love with the power of God's grace."

This reflects Ephesians 4:15, which tells us, "Speaking the truth in love, we will in all things grow up into him who is the Head, that is, Christ."

Timothy Keller goes on to say, "As a divine institution, marriage has several inherent powers that we must accept and use—the power of truth, the power of love, and the power of grace. These three powers will do their best work in us during times when we find it hard to love the semi-stranger to whom we are married."[37] The marriage relationship is different from all other relationships because it is within that relationship that all of our flaws, personality traits, and shortcomings come to light and drastically impact our relationship, simply because our spouse is more aware of those flaws than anyone we've ever been around. Keller gives this description:

> What are the flaws that your spouse will see? You may be a fearful person, with a tendency toward great anxiety. You may be a proud person, with a tendency to be opinionated and self-ish. You may be an inflexible person, with a tendency to be demanding and sulky if you don't get your way. You may be an abrasive or harsh person, who people tend to respect more than they love. You may be an undisciplined person, with a tendency to be unreliable and disorganized. You may be an oblivious person, who tends to be distracted, insensitive, and unaware of how you come across to others. You may be a perfectionist, with a tendency to be judgmental and critical of others and also to get down on yourself. You may be an impatient, irritable person, with a tendency to hold grudges or to lose your temper too often. You may be a highly independent person, who does not like to be responsible for the needs of others, who dislikes having to make joint decisions, and who most definitely hates to ask for any help yourself. You may be a person who wants far too much to be liked, and so you tend to shade the truth, you can't keep secrets, and you work too hard to please everyone. You may be thrifty but at the same time miserly with money, too unwilling to spend it on your own needs appropriately, and ungenerous to others. But while your character flaws may have created mild problems for other people, the will create major problems for your spouse and your marriage. For example, a tendency to hold grudges could be a problem within friendships, but within marriage it can kill the relationship.[38]

If you didn't see one character flaw from the above list in your own life, then read through the excerpt again. I would hope we can all acknowledge that we have blind spots in our own lives, and it is important for us to be open and honest in any and all relationships. Author and leadership expect John Maxwell gives this definition for a blind spot: "An area in someone's life in which he continually fails to see himself or his situation realistically. This unawareness often causes great damage to the person and those around him."[39] It is important to understand that marriage doesn't create your weaknesses—it reveals them! This is why marriage can bring out the worst in us. This does not need to be a bad thing, because this is how we can become a better person. This will help those who are Christ-followers to become more like Christ.

Timothy Keller says that marriage by its very nature has the "power of truth"—the power to show you the truth about who you are. He strongly states, "don't resist this power that marriage has." Not only does marriage have the power of truth, but it also has the "power of love." This can become an unmatched power to affirm you and heal you of the deepest wounds and hurts of your life. Keller states, "Marriage puts into your spouse's hand a massive power to reprogram your own self-appreciation. The love and affirmation of your spouse has the power to heal you of many of the deepest wounds."[40]

We will talk more about this in chapter 6, but the power of healing love in marriage is a miniature version of the same power that Jesus has *with* us. In Christ, God sees us as righteous, holy, and perfect:

"It is because of him that you are in Christ Jesus, who has become for us wisdom from God—that is, our righteousness, holiness and redemption" (1 Corinthians 1:30).

Keller rightly states,

> Truth without love ruins the oneness, and love without truth gives the illusion of unity but actually stops the journey and the growth. The solution is grace. The experience of Jesus' grace makes it possible to practice the two most important skills in marriage: forgiveness and repentance. Only if we are very good at forgiving and very good at repenting can truth and love be kept together.[41]

Your marriage can be revived or redeemed even if only one partner discovers that love isn't "That Lovin' Feeling"; rather, it is a "lovin' action" lived out no matter how we feel.

Feelings Are Legitimate: Love Lasts Forever

Paul ends the section in 1 Corinthians 13 with the words "love will last forever!" (verse 8). He then ends the chapter with, "Three things will last forever—faith, hope, and love—and the greatest of these is love" (verse 13). Paul does not make a frivolous statement here; love is the greatest of all and a choice that is available to all. It is important to begin to live out love by giving of yourself to another person in order to meet his or her basic needs without having any expectations in return. When you give of your time, effort, and attention to another person in order to meet his or her basic needs, then real love will begin to happen. You must understand that we need to give first before anything comes back in return. Even then it can take time, and you may not receive the return you hoped for. That type of "giving" love is the exact representation of the love God has given to us. You may be familiar with John 3:16, "God so loved the world," but it is important to also know 1 John 4:19, "We love because he first loved us."

A powerful definition of love is from John Piper's book *Desiring God*: "Love is the overflow of joy in God that gladly meets the needs of others."[42] Love is not merely the action of meeting others' needs; it includes the motive behind the action. True love knows God is love, and therefore we can love others. God is love, and love is from God. Therefore, loving others is doing whatever it takes for them to have as much of God as they can.

We can be absolutely confident and know how much God loves us, and also know that His love is not dependent on our love for Him. If we doubt God's love for us or feel that He doesn't love us, it doesn't mean that He loves us less or doesn't love us at all. His love was never dependent on what we do or how we feel. Love lies at the very core of God's nature ("God is love," 1 John 4:16). When that love, His love, touches you, you will discover there is nothing more powerful in the entire universe. It is more powerful than your failures, sins, disappointments, or even your fears. God knows that when you tap the depths of His love, your life will forever be changed. That love, His love, is available to each and every one of us: "God has poured out his love into our hearts by the Holy Spirit" (Romans 5:5). Don't miss these words: "God poured out his love into our hearts," and it is not dependent on us but on the Holy Spirit. We do not have to muster up enough love; we have to live in that love.

BEFORE YOU SAY I DON'T

The Bible speaks of love as a selfless active care and concern for another's well-being. Love is more about sacrifice and service than about having a warm feeling. Love builds up relationships; selfishness erodes relationships. Feelings can become self-centered, but love based on what you value about the relationship will help you find it easier to negotiate difficult times and disappointments. The Apostle Paul tells husbands to love their wives (Ephesians 5:25) and wives to love their husbands (Titus 2:4). Biblical love is seen primarily in choices, attitudes, and actions, not in emotions. No matter where you are, what you've done or failed to do, or how bad your circumstances are, Jesus is with you, and He loves you. None of us can survive without love, which is why we're called to love one another. If you need warmth, friendship, and love from others, take a risk: reach out and love your spouse with actions.

Timothy Keller says,

> Within this Christian vision of marriage, here's what it means to fall in love. It is to look at another person and get a glimpse of what God is creating, and to say, "I see who God is making you, and it excites me! I want to be part of that. I want to partner with you and God in the journey you are taking to his throne." And when we get there, I will look at your magnificence and say, "I always knew you could be like this. I got glimpses of it on earth, but now look at you!"[43]

Do not underestimate the impact of love. Following is a powerful blog post that speaks volumes about the impact of love in marriage and divorce.

How You Love Differently When You're a Child of Divorce-by Anna Bashedly (www.annabash. com/blog)[44]

> You never listen to people's words—you listen to their actions. Promises mean nothing to you, neither do intentions. You learned at a very young age that it's not the thought that counts. The "I love you" and "I miss you" and the "for better or for worse" don't mean a thing unless they're executed through actions: The being there or the showing up for someone. You don't care about the, "but baby deep down you know that I love you." No. People actually have to show you they care to win your heart.
>
> You don't flinch when people ask about your parents. You have memorized the script back and forth. You have dealt with trust issues for as long as you can remember. Yeah, you don't want the cliché labels: The one with abandonment issues. The one who keeps you at a distance. The one looking to fill a void. You don't need anyone's sympathy. You don't want anyone's pity—so you will always try to keep this part of you hidden, it's just a part of you, but a part that's still alive and well, comfortable in its home in your bones, a tiny inkling that you need to fight every time someone tries to get close to you nevertheless.
>
> At the same time, love scares you. When you finally start to feel safe with someone, you question it. How can you not? You've seen firsthand how even true love can break into a million pieces, bringing out the worst in people. How fireworks eventually combust, how commitment breaks like glass, how people promise to be there until "death do them part," for "better or for worse," but promises don't mean a thing. So you put up a shield you spent years crafting—it's

a strong shield, preparing you for the worst. Abandonment is your worst nightmare, because you've seen how no matter how much someone may love you, they can leave. And that is the most terrifying thing you have ever learned. If the one relationship you needed to work more than anything fell apart, it's fair game for any other relationship to break. For anyone else to decide it's not worth it. For anyone else to decide you're not worth it.

It broke your heart to see your parents in pain. You've seen them in their most vulnerable states—you've seen the fights leaving them burned and confused, so you've made a promise to never let yourself be in that state. No matter how much you love someone, you're incredibly uncomfortable letting them see your most vulnerable parts. You do it for protection.

When you do let someone in, it's hard for you to not try to control the relationship, to not have anxiety every time they don't respond to your calls when they're out—"Let it go. You're worrying for nothing" you reassure yourself. But anxiety always seems to win.

You have a big fear of the unknown. So you compensate. You're driven, you're unapologetic. You relish in your independence, you go after what you want—fearlessly, without caring about the approval of others. You will seem bulletproof. The people who have experienced the most pain always do. You know you can't control other people, but you also know that there's always a silver lining. Even the worst situation or event has a positive aspect. For you, it's your drive and empathy.

When you do love, you love unconditionally. You will give your partner all of your love and effort as a way to keep the flame alive. You want it to last. There's still a part of you that won't ever stop fighting for true love, a small part, but a part you'll do anything to hang on to nevertheless.

God's love has radically impacted our world. He wants to radically impact your world. God's love through you will impact your family. Live out God's love as Peter challenges us: "Most important of all, continue to show deep love for each other, for love covers a multitude of sins" (1 Peter 4:8). That love is not only for you, but for you to extend to others.

Recounting Real Relationships

(This is a family that I know, but they have requested to remain anonymous)

What I wonder the most, is, would I have the insight I have on my marriage and divorce if he had not ended his life? We were so well matched that people who met us separately and did not know that we were dating tried to set us up with each other. We were best friends. We spent seven years together and only a handful of days apart. We could work together, travel together, play together, laugh together. But, five years in...alcohol.

We were not followers of Christ, and making a living was a challenge, and we had some silly disagreements about who cleaned what and how the money was spent...which really was just on bills. Money began to disappear, he began to lose job after job, his health began to slide rapidly, and I did not know what to do. He was never happy anymore, and sending him to the doctor was creating a large debt, which would have been fine if the doctors were finding what was wrong. He slept all the time, and his mood was changing. He would fall over while standing on the deck smoking a cigarette. I thought maybe he was losing his mind, until one day I took a drink from his water bottle. The truth that I had never considered was that he was hiding gin and vodka in his water bottles.

For nearly a year after that discovery, we worked toward his sobriety, but I felt that every step forward caused him to go further into the disease. I had already lost him, and I convinced myself that I was the toxic person in the relationship and that, if I removed myself, he would get better again and live a happy life. So, he left. He begged to come home, and I said no. I worked hard to remind myself that I was not healthy for him, and he eventually went to live with his parents in another state. Our divorce was basically executed over the phone. Shortly after the divorce, we stopped talking. I decided that he was better this way, and I believed that he had found the help he needed and was sober.

Eight years later, a letter found its way to me from his mother, to tell me that he had ended his life after years of homeless shelters and rehab facilities. The news of his death shattered me into numbness. It meant that I had been wrong. He had never gotten better. It meant that I did not even come close to saving his life by removing myself. I found out from another woman who dated him shortly after he left me that he had tried to slit his wrists at that time. I discovered through his mother and this woman that he still cried for me when certain songs came on the radio or when he saw things that reminded him of me. This was a reality that I have never allowed myself to consider over the years...that he still loved me.

I was not whole after he left. I was more broken than I ever allowed myself to realize. After he had gone (and was still alive), I dated a string of men that were varying degrees of awful to and for me. In retrospect, I feel that I had been punishing myself for failing my husband and my marriage. How could I be allowed to feel a love like that again? I did not feel that I could be trusted to nurture a relationship with a kind and good man.

I came to follow Christ about eight months after his death. What would have been if we had found Christ together? Why had I not tried harder to find a solution for him, to fight harder for his life and our marriage? Would he have ever accepted Christ into his heart? I wish I had been mature enough in Christ way back when I was married to have known there were options for us. I wish that we had had friends at that time that were bold enough to suggest we seek the counsel of a pastor. We were both very stubborn: he did not really want to choose to live, and I was not strong enough on my own to fight for both of our lives. Christ has made beauty from ashes on this for me...but my heart is forever changed by the man I truly loved and lost, and I am hesitant to enter another earthly relationship.

Journey Together
Marriage Workbook

1) What are some emotions that, if expressed, can destroy a marriage? How can emotions like anger and bitterness grow and hinder a relationship? (Read Ephesians 4:26 and Hebrews 12:15.)

_____

_____

_____

2) Discuss what John Piper's quote as stated in this chapter means to you: "Love is the overflow of joy in God that gladly meets the needs of others."

_____

_____

_____

3) What does Timothy Keller's quote in this chapter tell us about marrying the right person in regards to love as discussed in this chapter?

"We never know whom we marry, we just think we do. Or even if we first marry the right person, just give it a while, he or she will change. For marriage that means we are not the same person after we have entered it. The primary problem is...learning how to love and care for the stranger to whom you find yourself married."

_____

_____

_____

4) In his book *The Grace and Truth Paradox*, Randy Alcorn says, "Truth without grace breeds self-righteousness and legalism. Grace without truth breeds deception and moral compromise. The key

to true Christian spirituality is to integrate these two qualities into life, imitating the character of Christ."[45] In what ways do you see love, truth, and grace helping in your marriage?

_____

_____

_____

5) Our ability to be gracious flows from recognizing how much God has done for us and how little we deserve it. How does Timothy Keller's statement as quoted in this chapter reflect that?

Truth without love ruins the oneness, and love without truth gives the illusion of unity but actually stops the journey and the growth. The solution is grace. The experience of Jesus' grace makes it possible to practice the two most important skills in marriage: forgiveness and repentance. Only if we are very good at forgiving and very good at repenting can truth and love be kept together

(Read: Ephesians 2:4–5, 8–9; 2 Corinthians 12:8–9; Colossians 3:12–14.)

_____

_____

_____

6) Reread the article in this chapter by Anna Bash: "How You Love Differently when You're a Child of Divorce." What insights did you gain from this?

_____

_____

_____

7) How can Peter's words impact how we respond when someone sins again us? "Most important of all, continue to show deep love for each other, for love covers a multitude of sins" (1 Peter 4:8).

_____

_____

_____

PRAY

Here is a prayer to get you started, and remember: it's not the words that matter so much as what's in your heart. Allow Paul's prayer to be your prayer. Read it out loud:

"I pray that you, being rooted and established in love, may have power...to grasp how wide and long and high and deep is the love of Christ...that you may be filled to the measure of all the fullness of God" (Ephesians 3:17–19).

God, I want to know you and your love, and I ask you to show me how to love through my actions even when I don't feel like it. In Jesus's Name, Amen

CHAPTER 5
Faith Doesn't Take a Leap

*"Marriage is an institution that existed before governments existed.
It's something that reflects nature and reflects God and God's will for us.
And both from the standpoint of faith and reason it makes all the sense in the world.
And it's beneficial for society."*
RICK SANTORUM

A guy sees a sign in front of a house: "Talking Dog for Sale." He rings the bell, and the owner tells him the dog is in the backyard. The guy goes into the backyard and sees a black mutt just sitting there. "You talk?" he asks.

"Sure do." the dog replies.

"So, what's your story?"

The dog looks up and says, "Well, I discovered my gift of talking pretty young, and I wanted to help the government, so I told the CIA about my gift, and in no time, they had me jetting from country to country, sitting in rooms with spies and world leaders, because no one figured a dog would be eavesdropping. I was one of their most valuable spies eight years running.

"The jetting around really tired me out, and I knew I wasn't getting any younger, and I wanted to settle down. So I signed up for a job at the airport to do some undercover security work, mostly wandering near suspicious characters and listening in. I uncovered some incredible dealings there and was awarded a batch of medals. I had a wife, a mess of puppies, and now I'm just retired."

The guy is amazed. He goes back in and asks the owner what he wants for the dog.

The owner says, "Ten dollars."

The guy says, "This dog is amazing. Why on earth are you selling him so cheap?"

"Cause he's a liar. He didn't do any of that stuff!"

We are living in a time when it is really hard to know who or what to believe. Who can we trust? Who can we put our faith in? I am writing this chapter one week following the 2016 presidential election, and the talk is about who you can trust or who you can put your faith in. People are protesting, and in some cases rioting in the streets, about a constitutional election because things didn't work out the way they wanted, or because they don't trust the one who was elected. The question we all must answer is "in whom do I trust?" or in whom have i put my faith in?"

If you are familiar with the 1989 film *Indiana Jones and the Last Crusade*, then you know that Indiana Jones was forced to pass through three challenges in order to reach the Holy Grail and save his father from death. These tests were designed to prevent the faithless from reaching the cup. Dr. Jones, Indy's dad, had uncovered ancient material that described these perils, and he had recorded them in a diary. In order to succeed, Indiana had to decipher the riddles in the diary to make it through the maze of dangers, or die in the process.

The last trial before he could enter the inner room containing the grail was the leap of faith. From Indy's perspective, he was stepping out into thin air over a deep chasm. But the prospect of losing his father motivated him to make the leap. As you saw in the movie, amazingly, he was caught by a ledge that was camouflaged from anyone trying to cross! He had firm ground to walk upon! His blind step of faith saved his father's life, but it had to start with a step.

Faith Is Foundational in All Areas of Life—Including Marriage

Everyone, absolutely everyone, lives by faith. Unlike Indiana Jones, our faith does not have to be blind, and there is no reason to take a leap, but we do have to take a step. That step of faith can not only save your marriage but might just save a lot of hurt and heartache for you, your family, and even your friends. If we understand that each and every one of us operates based on various faith assumptions, then that will at least begin to open the doors toward a dialogue about how to live our lives and how to fix our lives. To be honest, my hope is to make a clear case for the belief system I have put my faith in: the Good News of Jesus Christ. Getting married and developing a healthy marriage are not easy for anyone. Therefore, to ask and seek the One who I believe established marriage can only help make it what His desire was from the beginning.

Having a personal relationship with Jesus Christ begins with a step of faith that will impact your life. It is faith in a God who loves you, knows you, and wants the best for you that will drastically help you better engage and understand one another. The Apostle Paul talks about a battle we are in with an enemy, the father of lies (John 8:44). The Bible remind us, "Our fight is not against people on earth but against the rulers and authorities and the powers of this world's darkness, against the spiritual powers of evil in the heavenly world" (Ephesians 6:12, NCV). It can be life changing to know that your marital problems are not against your spouse but are spiritual in nature—and therefore, your faith in an all-mighty, all-knowing, and all-powerful God will make all the difference. Marriage is the spiritual union of two souls to serve the highest good and create a family. From the beginning, evil spiritual forces have tried to destroy marriage and family (Genesis 3). Even today—through no-fault divorce laws, cohabitation, and same-sex marriage—this evil spiritual battle continues in our society.

Timothy Keller says that, knowingly or unknowingly, we all live according to a worldview (how we see the world around us) that seeks answers to these three questions:

1. How are things supposed to be?
2. What is the main problem with things as they are?
3. What is the solution, and how can it be realized?[46]

Everybody has an answer to those questions—whether it's a clear answer or something that's understood without being stated—and we all live our lives according to how we answer those questions. The answers to those questions are extremely relevant when it comes to marriage and how healthy your marriage is. Everyone lives by faith, not just those who are religious or who are Christians. Everyone always trusts and puts their faith in something to secure and satisfy them in this life.

Focus on *Who* Your Faith Is In

The Apostle Paul says, "For we walk by faith, not by sight" (2 Corinthians 5:7). Your heart is designed to contain God, and God wants to live inside you. The Bible tells us that there is a God-shaped vacuum in our hearts; there is a hole in our hearts that only God can fill. We were made to be connected to our Creator. We were made to know Him and to be plugged into His power. Solomon says, "Yet God has made everything beautiful for its own time. He has planted eternity in the human heart, but even so, people cannot see the whole scope of God's work from beginning to end" (Ecclesiastes 3:11). Sadly, too many spend their lives looking for something other than God to fill their longing for meaning and purpose in life. But in pursuing anything else in life but God—things that are not eternal—people remain unfulfilled, and they wonder why their lives never seem satisfactory.

It has been said that faith is only as good as the object in which it is placed. Christian Pastor and writer Walter Martin says, "All faith is subsumed under the overarching biblical doctrine of the sovereignty of God." The Creator is the Lord of the universe, not a cosmic "gofer" at the beck and call of His creation. It is not our faith that sits on the throne, but our sovereign God. If we think of faith in terms of taking a leap of faith, then we would be committing to a decision, person, or course of action with very little or no information or assurances. That most certainly would be a blind or even ignorant faith that would make little to no difference in your life. Anytime we demonstrate faith, we're relying on something. When you sit in a chair, you're trusting that the chair's manufacturer produced something that will hold you up. When you're on the freeway, you're relying on your car and every other driver around you to keep you safe. When you visit the doctor, you're relying on his or her expertise and knowledge to make you well.

This concept is important when it comes to marriage, because when you're married, you need to rely on the Creator and author of marriage. To put your faith in the God of the Bible means you rely on Him and depend on His reliability—not on your own or your spouse's, and not on your circumstances. Having faith means realizing that God is bigger, greater, and better than you—and oh, by the way, he cares about you and loves you greatly.

Faith is having to place your trust in the knowledge that someone is much bigger than you and plays a role in your destiny. Proverbs 14:12 says, "There is a path before each person that seems right, but it ends in death." That's the problem with relying on yourself. Humans are often wrong. We don't know what the future holds. We are not God! Faith is an admission that neither you nor any other human being or entity is completely in control of all the things that go on around you. That should bring us to a faith in the One that we can trust and lean on when it comes to marriage and marriage problems, because marriage is God's idea.

Author and Pastor Max Lucado said, "God created marriage. No government subcommittee envisioned it. No social organization developed it. Marriage was conceived and born in the mind of God."

A person who has biblical faith is someone who draws strength, comfort and hope from the knowledge that something is greater than them—God—and He gives them purpose in the world. It's just a way of not only understanding their world, but coming to terms with life, death, and everything in between. Hebrews 11:1 tells us, "Now faith is being sure of what we hope for and certain of what we do not see." Faith demands an object, as it must have something or someone to trust.

By putting your trust and faith in God, you can become a person who can receive all that the Lord wants for your marriage. Start walking and talking in faith! It will take time, but start by taking baby steps, and you will become stronger in your faith every day! Notice what Jesus says about our faith:

"Have faith in God," Jesus answered. "I tell you the truth, if anyone says to this mountain, 'Go, throw yourself into the sea,' and does not doubt in his heart but believes that what he says will happen, it will be done for him. Therefore I tell you, whatever you ask for in prayer, believe that you have received it, and it will be yours. And when you stand praying, if you hold anything against anyone, forgive him, so that your Father in heaven may forgive you your sins." (Mark 11:22–25)

Faith is totally depending on God and being willing to do His will in your marriage. It is complete and humble obedience to God's will and way in your life. Faith is believing and trusting in your heart and mind that God's promises are true and Christ's work is complete.

Pastor and author Larry Osborne says, "The kind of faith the Bible advocates and God wants from us has far more to do with our actions than our feelings. In fact, biblical faith is so closely tied to actions of obedience that the Bible ridicules the very idea of someone claiming to have faith without acting upon it."[47] In a sermon that Larry Osborne preached in regards to faith said, "Faith is trusting God enough to follow Him. The opposite of faith is inactivity, not fear or doubt."[48] The Bible is very clear that Biblical faith is not passive, but always involves action:

"In the same way, faith by itself, if it is not accompanied by action, is dead. But someone will say, "You have faith; I have deeds." Show me your faith without deeds, and I will show you my faith by what I do. You believe that there is one God. Good! Even the demons believe that--and shudder. You foolish man, do you want evidence that faith without deeds is useless? Was not our ancestor Abraham considered righteous for what he did when he offered his son Isaac on the altar? You see that his faith and his actions were working together, and his faith was made complete by what he did." (James 2:17-22)

To receive salvation, we are told to "believe in the Lord Jesus, and you will be saved" (Acts 16:31a). For the unbeliever, faith in Christ is exercised with a view to receiving a benefit, and that benefit is Christ living in you from now to eternity (John 3:16). To be clear, faith does not save; God saves! Faith is merely the means by which the unsaved person receives salvation, as God alone does the saving. Though we may exercise faith and receive a benefit, the object always gets the credit, and in the case of our salvation, God alone gets the glory.

God is always faithful to his word:

- "God wanted to prove that his promise was true to those who would get what he promised. And he wanted them to understand clearly that his purposes never change, so he made an oath. These two things cannot change: God cannot lie when he makes a promise, and he cannot lie when he makes an oath. These things encourage us who came to God for safety. They give us strength to hold on to the hope we have been given. We have this hope as an anchor for the soul, sure and strong" (Hebrews 6:17–19, NCV).
- "God, who has called you into fellowship with his Son Jesus Christ our Lord, is faithful" (1 Corinthians 1:9).
- "No temptation has seized you except what is common to man. And God is faithful; he will not let you be tempted beyond what you can bear. But when you are tempted, he will also provide a way out so you can stand up under it" (1 Corinthians 10:13).
- "The Lord is faithful, and he will strengthen and protect you from the evil one" (2 Thessalonians 3:3).
- "If we confess our sins, he is faithful and just and will forgive us our sins and purify us from all unrighteousness" (1 John 1:9).

The key to keeping faith in a faithful God and avoiding divorce is not to avoid divorce; it is to thrive in marriage, being confident that God is for you and your marriage. For that to happen, you need to be as fully invested in your marriage as you are in your faith. Believe in it. Trust in it. Know it will guide you and protect you. Remind yourself of how far you've come and how much you've already overcome. Look forward to how far there is to go together and how much more there is to experience. Consider how you got here and why you came in the first place. Then let go and let faith guide the rest of your journey through marriage, family, and life.

Freedom to Live by Faith, "But If Not"

Contrary to what some believe, the Christian faith is one of freedom, not bondage. The Apostle Paul says, "Christ has set us free to live a free life. So take your stand! Never again let anyone put a harness of slavery on you" (Galatians 5:1, MSG). Biblical faith gives us a freedom we could never know apart from a relationship with Christ. Fear, guilt, shame, and having to prove yourself to be accepted is driven by the world we live in and was never about biblical Christianity. Our faith sets us free, and one of the more well-known Old Testament stories reveals how we have the freedom to live by faith, "but if not," we are to still live by faith.

Shadrach, Meshach and Abednego were thrown into the fiery furnace because they wouldn't budge, wouldn't bow, and then wouldn't burn. They didn't have any doubt of God's power:

Shadrach, Meshach and Abednego answered and said to the king, "O Nebuchadnezzar, we have no need to answer you in this matter. If that is the case, our God whom we serve is able to deliver us from the burning fiery furnace and He will deliver us from your hand, O king. **But** *if not*, let it be known to you, O king, that we do not serve your gods, nor will we worship the gold image which you have set up." (Daniel 3:16–18)

Let me ask you a question. Does your faith have an "if not" clause in it? "Our God is able to deliver us." That is the faith we are to place in our God, and it is the faith that God gives us as we continue to trust Him. By putting their faith in their God, Shadrach, Meshach, and Abednego refused to follow the way of the world and responded with some of the most inspiring and faithful words in all of Scripture:

1) "Our God...**is** able to deliver us"
2) "He **will** deliver us from your hand"
3) "But if not..."

The third proclamation speaks three powerful words of a strong and prevailing faith. When facing trials, tests, and tribulations, do you have the kind of faith to respond as the three young Hebrew boys did? We know, according to scripture, there was a fourth man in the fire...and it was Jesus! What a lesson for us. God is always with us, and He promises to never leave or forsake us (Hebrews 13:5). The story ends with Shadrach, Meshach, and Abednego being released from the fiery furnace unharmed. "But if not," their faith was still grounded and founded in the God!

I cannot promise this is how your life or your marriage will end, but I do know we can have a faith that we can stand on in the face of reality even though we go through a fire. *God is able to deliver us from the burning, fiery furnace!* We need a faith that is always subject to the divine will of God. We need a faith that will be committed to God, regardless of the outcome. God doesn't promise to save us from the flames, but He has promised to be with us as we walk through the fire. Faith is not primarily receiving from God what you want. It is accepting from God what He gives: "Now faith is being sure of what we hope for and certain of what we do not see. And without faith it is impossible to please God, because anyone who comes to him must believe that he exists and that he rewards those who earnestly seek him" (Hebrews 11:1–6).

Marriage is so much more than a license, a ceremony, or a promise made with symbolic jewelry. Marriage is the spiritual union of two souls who have been guided to each other to serve the highest good and create a spiritual family. The exchange of vows is a sacred rite of passage whose true meaning has escaped so many. When the ideals and fantasy of what you imagine marriage to be feels like it is beginning to fade, then the realities of responsibility set in, and your emotional and spiritual health may take a back seat. At that point, divorce may seem an attractive option to stop the fights and end the suffering.

If your marriage is in trouble, and you're starting to doubt the decisions you've made, take a step back and take a deep breath. Close your eyes and remember that there is always somewhere to turn when you feel you've lost your way. Put your faith in a faithful and trustworthy God, as He will give you strength and clarity. He is able to change your mind, your heart, and your spirit so you can create a wonderful marriage that you want and can enjoy.

Recounting Real Relationships
A Roomful of Yearning and Regret[49]

Not long ago, the friend of a friend spent the night in a hotel room, which is sometimes what you do when you find out your spouse has been having a year-long affair. His flight was sadly predictable—it's all many of us are capable of after discovering such a betrayal—though I am sure he now realizes that mere movement is not a fix for that kind of agony.

I know this for two reasons: No. 1, I have had an affair; No. 2, I have been the victim of one. When you unfurl these two experiences in the sunlight for comparison, and measure their worth and pain, the former is only marginally better than the latter. And both, frankly, are awful.

I recently offered my cheated-upon view of things to my acquaintance, who has returned every night for a week to that hotel because he cannot bear to look at his wife. A couple of years ago I offered the other side to a friend when she was considering having an affair.

Start, I suggested to her, by picturing yourself in the therapist's office with your betrayed husband after you've been found out (and you will be found out). You will hear yourself saying you cheated because your needs weren't being met. The spark was gone. You were bored in your marriage. Your lover understands you better. One or another version of this excuse will cross your lips like some dark, knee-jerk Hallmark-card sentiment.

I'm not saying these feelings aren't legitimate, just that they don't legitimize what you're doing. If you believed they did, your stomach wouldn't drop on your way out the door to your lover. You wouldn't feel the need to shower before climbing into the marital bed after a liaison. You wouldn't feel like a train had struck you in the back when your son asked why you forgot his lacrosse game the other day.

When you miss a family function because of work, you get over it. When you miss a family function because you were in a hotel room with your lover, you feel breathless with misery. The great sex, by the way, is a given. When you have an affair you already know you will have passionate sex—the urgency, newness and illicit nature of the affair practically guarantee that. What you don't know, or perhaps what you don't allow yourself to think about, is that your life will become an unbearable mix of yearning and regret because of it. It will be difficult if not impossible to be in any one place with contentment.

This is no way for an adult to live. When you're with your lover, you'll be working on your alibi and feeling loathsome. When you're with your spouse, you'll be dying to return to your love nest. When you are at home, everything in your life will look just a little bit out of register—the furniture, the food in your refrigerator, your children, your dog—because you've detached yourself from your normal point of reference, and it now belongs to a reality you've abandoned.

You will be pulled between two poles, one of obligation and responsibility, the other of pleasure and escape, and the stress of these opposing forces will threaten to split you in two.

I met the man I cheated with early in my marriage. He was the beautiful twin brother of a friend, something like a young Errol Flynn. I was entranced. My husband traveled a lot and I took advantage of that, finding myself at my lover's apartment often. But at home with my husband during those ragged months, I was anxious and ill at ease. I should have been focusing on our new house, our new jobs, but my inability to resist the pull of the affair ruined all of that. I could not concentrate on our coupled life and frankly did not care to.

I knew I needed to stop it, but didn't have the will to do so on my own. I had to enlist my husband, to tell him so that we could battle this together. So I admitted to the affair one evening after dinner. Almost 20 years after that confession I can still remember how the whole world narrowed down to the two of us sitting there, that new truth congealing between us.

Once the affair is out in the open, you will strive mightily to justify yourself. You will begin many sentences with the phrase, "I never meant to _____" But one look at the hollow-eyed, defeated form of your spouse will remind you that such a claim is beside the point. You can both get over this, yes. But the innocence will have gone out of your union and it will seem as if a bone has been broken and healed, but one that rain or cold weather can set to throbbing again.

So, now take the other side. You discover your cheating spouse, as I once did, and what you experience is not far removed from posttraumatic stress. It is a form of shock. As your mind struggles to accommodate this wrenching reality, you won't be able to sleep or focus. Your fight-or-flight mechanism will go haywire. You will become consumed with where your spouse is at any moment, even if you see him in the pool with your children.

You will lose your appetite. Stress will blow out your metabolism. You will torture yourself with details known and imagined. You will fit together the mysteries of his daily patterns like a wicked puzzle. Every absence or unexplained late night or new habit or sudden urge to join a gym, for instance, will suddenly make horrible sense. You will wonder why you were so stupid.

But as the writer Paul Theroux says in one of his travelogues, "It is very easy to plant a bomb in a peaceful, trusting place." That is what the cheating spouse has done. Then detonated it. Sooner or later your illicit, once-beloved object of affection will become tawdry, wearying. You will come to long for simple, honest pleasures like making dinner with your sons or going out to the movies without having to look over your shoulder.

On the other side, your spouse's philandering will cease to torment you and instead the whole episode will leave you disgusted and bored and desirous to get out. You will just want to be with someone who does what he says he is going to do, goes where he says he is going to go, and can be found any time you need him because he is not hiding. I say all this by way of hope, believe it or not. Affairs are one of the adult world's few disasters that can be gotten over, with a lot of time and kindness. It has to burn out of you over months and months, flaming up and then subsiding as you get used to the fact.

A great deal of comfort will come from your friends, many of whom will offer advice—hate him, leave him, move on—that you should listen to politely and then reject. After all, the consequences of your decisions will be visited upon you, not your friends. They will be only too happy to amplify your confusion, listen to you cry, and then get into the car and drive home to their own intact families.

In the end your marriage may not need to be trashed, though mine was. The affairs metastasized in our relationship from the inside out. By the time all was said and done, there was little left to save. Our marriage had become like a leaf eaten away by caterpillars, where the petiole and midrib remain with some ghostly connective tracery in between. Not enough to hold even a drop of rain.

I look at my parents and at how much simpler their lives are at the ages of 75, mostly because they haven't marred the landscape with grand-scale deceit. They have this marriage of 50-some years behind them, and it is a monument to success. A few weeks or months of illicit passion could not hold a candle to it.

If you imagine yourself in such a situation, where would you fit an affair in neatly? If you were 75, which would you rather have: years of steady if occasionally strained devotion, or something that looks a little bit like the Iraqi city of Fallujah, cratered with spent artillery?

From where I stand now, it all just looks like a cheap hotel room, whether you're in that room to have an affair or to escape from the discovery of one. And despite the sex and the excitement, or the drama and the fix of everyone's empathetic attention, there is no view from this room that is worth having.

Journey Together
Marriage Workbook

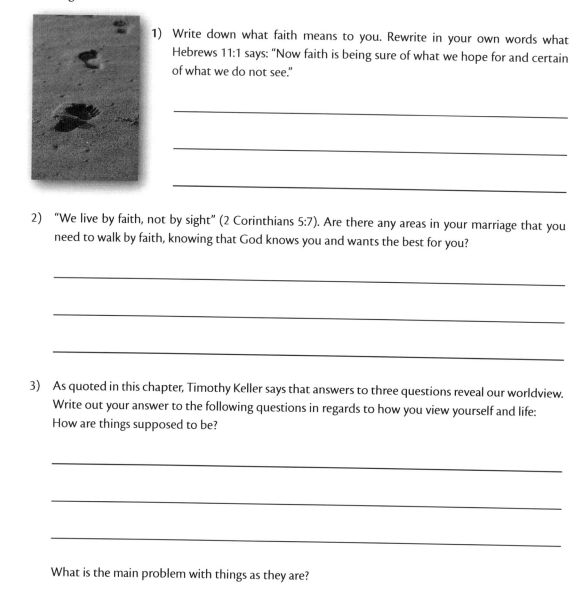

1) Write down what faith means to you. Rewrite in your own words what Hebrews 11:1 says: "Now faith is being sure of what we hope for and certain of what we do not see."

_____

_____

_____

2) "We live by faith, not by sight" (2 Corinthians 5:7). Are there any areas in your marriage that you need to walk by faith, knowing that God knows you and wants the best for you?

_____

_____

_____

3) As quoted in this chapter, Timothy Keller says that answers to three questions reveal our worldview. Write out your answer to the following questions in regards to how you view yourself and life: How are things supposed to be?

_____

_____

_____

What is the main problem with things as they are?

_____

_____

_____

What is the solution, and how can it be realized?

_____

BEFORE YOU SAY I DON'T

_____

_____

4) What do Solomon's words mean to you? "He has planted eternity in the human heart, but even so, people cannot see the whole scope of God's work from beginning to end" (Ecclesiastes 3:11). How do Solomon's words in Proverbs 14:12 relate to the verse in Ecclesiastes?

_____

_____

_____

5) What do the following verses say about God's faithfulness?
- Hebrews 6:17–19
- 1 Corinthians 1:9
- 1 Corinthians 10:13
- 2 Thessalonians 3:3
- 1 John 1:9
- 2 Timothy 2:13

_____

_____

_____

6) What do the following verses say about our faith?
- Hebrews 11:1
- Mark 11:22–25
- Galatians 5:6
- 1 Peter 1:7

_____

_____

_____

7) We see throughout the scriptures that faith is proven by action. That is the difference between professing faith and possessing faith. What action steps can you take today to be faithful to God and your spouse through acts of kindness?

_____

_____

_____

8) Have you put your faith in Jesus Christ? The prayer of salvation is the most important prayer we'll ever pray. When you are ready to become a Christ-follower, acknowledge these components:
   1. Acknowledge that Jesus Christ is God.
   2. Confess your life of sin.
   3. Admit you are ready to trust Jesus Christ as our Savior and Lord.
   4. Ask Jesus to come into your heart, and ask Him to begin to live through you. Paul says, "If you confess with your mouth that Jesus is Lord and believe in your heart that God raised him from the dead, you will be saved. For it is by believing in your heart that you are made right with God, and it is by confessing with your mouth that you are saved" (Romans 10:9–10, NLT).

> Prayer of salvation: Father, I know that my sins have separated me from You. I am truly sorry, and now I want to turn away from my past sinful life toward You. Please forgive me. I believe that Your Son, Jesus Christ, died for my sins, was resurrected from the dead, and is alive, and I put my faith in Him. I invite Jesus to become the Lord of my life, to rule and reign in my heart from this day forward. Please send your Holy Spirit to help me follow You and to do Your will in my life. In Jesus's Name I pray, Amen.

PRAY

Here is a prayer to get you started, and remember: it's not the words that matter so much as what's in your heart. Make this your prayer to continuously live by faith. Read it out loud:

> Heavenly Father, You have promised that if I offer You a miniscule amount of faith, You will create something so much bigger out of it. Today, I offer You my faith in Your ability to bring Jesus into this marriage. I believe that You breathed life into Adam and made Eve from his rib. I believe that You, O Lord, can turn my bitterness into kindness. You can transform my self-focused stubbornness into a "your needs come first" mindset. You are able to restore us completely and allow our marriage to point others to Your perfect love for imperfect people. Let my faith become sight, Lord. In Jesus's Name, Amen

CHAPTER 6

Future Can Be Determined Today

"Never be afraid to trust an unknown future to a known God."
CORRIE TEN BOOM

A young woman brought her fiancé home to meet her parents for Thanksgiving dinner. After dinner, her mother told her father to find out about the young man. The father invited the fiancé to his study for a talk.

"So what are your plans?" the father asked the young man.

"I am a biblical scholar," he replied.

"A biblical scholar. Hmm," the father said. "Admirable, but what will you do to provide a nice house for my daughter to live in?"

"I will study," the young man replied, "and God will provide for us."

"And how will you buy her a beautiful engagement ring, such as she deserves?" asked the father.

"I will concentrate on my studies," the young man replied. "God will provide for us."

"And children?" asked the father. "How will you support children?"

"Don't worry, sir, God will provide," replied the fiancé.

The conversation proceeded like this, and each time the father questioned, the young idealist insisted that God would provide.

Later, the mother asked, "How did it go, honey?"

The father answered, "He has no job and no plans, and he thinks I'm God!"

The first step in restoring your marriage is to admit that you cannot manage or control your marriage, your spouse, or your own problems. This means you need to recognize the ineffectiveness of your attempts to change your and your spouse's faults and character defects. It is important to come to a place where you are willing to admit that the strategies you have tried have not worked and that every attempt you make to change or control your situation has failed. The things we do or work at *might* change things temporarily, but they usually will not last or result in permanent change. Real change can only begin to happen when you recognize that you are not in control, but you can trust that *God* is. When God becomes your focus, then your eyes are not on you, your spouse, your children, your career, or your money, but are on God and His love and grace. When we allow God to be God of our relationships, it means that we must learn to leave our spouse in God's hands and trust Him to work on our spouse's heart and soul as only He can. This is where prayer and the power of prayer can drastically change not only what God does in our spouse's heart, but more importantly in our own heart.

Whatever condition your marriage is in, God is in the business of performing miracles, transforming lives, and healing broken relationships. If God can bring dead people back to life (see Lazarus and Jesus), then He is able to bring life and breath back into your marriage. Your future can be bright because God is the light of the world. The Apostle Paul reminds us of that truth: "We saw how powerless we were to help ourselves; but that was good, for we put everything into the hands of God who alone could save us" (2 Corinthians 1:9). Don't miss what is said here: "We are powerless, and we need to put everything into God's hands!"

> I HAVE BEEN CRUCIFIED WITH CHRIST, IT IS NO LONGER I WHO LIVE BUT CHRIST WHO LIVES IN ME.
> Galatians 2:20

Choose Today to Live in Christ

The principles of this chapter have come to me personally through over thirty years of learning, ministering, teaching, and counseling many who have been through a wide variety of challenges in life, including dealing with divorce. Through this journey of learning, I have been impacted by a life-changing truth of understanding who I am in Christ. Whether through challenges I have faced in ministry, relationships, and family or from the books I've read over the years, God has given me insight and wisdom into the understanding that Christ lives in me, and I no longer live. I am continually learning and trusting that my life, my decision, and my future are best lived out when I am trusting Jesus to call the shots no matter what! It cannot be about me taking control, me trying harder, me doing more, but about me allowing Christ to live in me. That's the walk that we are to walk in the power and presence of the Holy Spirit: "But the fruit of the Spirit is love, joy, peace, patience, kindness, goodness, faithfulness, gentleness and self-control. Against such things there is no law. Those who belong to Christ Jesus have crucified the sinful nature with its passions and desires. Since we live by the Spirit, let us keep in step with the Spirit" (Galatians 5:22–25).

This journey of understanding Christ in you cannot be fully found in the pages of this of other books about who we are in Christ. It lies in the Father's heart and your own spiritual growth. The life of *Christ in you* is far better lived than it is read about.

My hope and prayer is these insights will challenge, encourage, and lead you to a lifelong freedom from the frustration of trying to prove yourself to anyone or *trying* to be a better person or Christian— because you can't do so through your own power or performance.

This truth came to me early in my ministry through Dann Spader, founder of Sonlife Ministries. He taught this simple but profound statement: "The Christian life is impossible—you can't do it. But the Christian life is simple—it's Christ living through you." The turning point came when it was lived out in my own ministry and friendship with the pastor's son, who was part of the student ministry in Iowa. Because of his own spiritual battles, I was introduced to Neil Anderson's book *The Bondage Breaker*. I cannot stress the importance of understanding this truth, which I believe comes from the very breath of God and is the heartbeat of His Word through the Apostle Paul. The phrase "in Christ" is used around 130 times in

Paul's thirteen epistles. It was not a divine anticipation on the part of Paul, but a very radical and definite experience.

Here are a few examples of that: "This is the mystery," Paul advises the Colossians: "Christ in you, the hope of glory" (Colossians 1:27). Paul also questions the Corinthians: "Do you not recognize that Jesus Christ is in you—unless you fail the test?" (2 Corinthians 13:5). "It is no longer I who live," he explains to the Galatians, "but Christ lives in me" (Galatians 2:20).

This particular verse in Galatians has been a personal life source many times in my marriage, my ministry, and the many difficult relationships and situations I've experienced in life. I encourage you to meditate on this truth on a regular basis, especially when you feel the need to have to prove yourself: "I have been crucified with Christ and I no longer live, but Christ lives in me. The life I live in the body, I live by faith in the Son of God, who loved me and gave himself for me" (Galatians 2:20).

Take time to read the following verses with an open heart and with your eyes wide open, believing that your life is not yours but it is God's:

- We have "all things in Christ" (1 Corinthians 3:21–23).
- "His divine power has given us everything we need for life and godliness" (2 Peter 1:3).
- "Every spiritual blessing in heavenly places in Christ Jesus" (Ephesians 1:3).
- We are "complete in Christ" (Colossians 2:10).

Everything that God wants us to have for everything that He wants to do in us is accorded to us by the indwelling presence and function of the living Lord Jesus. Your self-image will determine how you treat others, especially those you care about the most. Your identity in Christ means that when God looks at you, He see you as perfect, holy, and pure.

The choice to live in Christ was a critical piece in my own marriage. Through thirty years of marriage and counseling others, I have written out twelve basic principles that can help develop healthy marriages:

1. Your own security and significance come from *who you are* in Christ, not in or from your spouse. Keep God at the center of your marriage. Always keep your focus on Him, and on helping your spouse become more like Christ. (Dr. Larry Crabb: *The Marriage Builder* or www.newwayministries.org)
2. Marriage is God's idea, not man's; therefore, He knows what's best. You can trust Him to do what's best at all times.
3. Marriage is worth the investment, but you have to *invest* in your marriage for it to be worth the investment. It takes work!
4. Choosing your marriage partner is the most important human decision you will ever make.
5. Most fights are over stupid things that don't matter. Choose your battles. There are many things that are not worth the fight!
6. Most arguments are resolved when both people are more concerned with being in a healthy relationship rather than with *being right.*
7. Sex is essential to a marriage relationship. I am not making this up it is actually in the Bible: 1 Corinthians 7:2-5, "But because there is so much sexual immorality, each man should have

his own wife, and each woman should have her own husband. The husband should fulfill his wife's sexual needs, and the wife should fulfill her husband's needs. The wife gives authority over her body to her husband, and the husband gives authority over his body to his wife. Do not deprive each other of sexual relations, unless you both agree to refrain from sexual intimacy for a limited time so you can give yourselves more completely to prayer. Afterward, you should come together again so that Satan won't be able to tempt you because of your lack of self-control."

I understand that not all husbands or wives are sexually driven, but a mutual understanding of this aspect of a marriage must be made clear especially in our culture of sexual promiscuity, computers and pornography.

8. Kids are awesome, but emphasize your marriage. Children are only a gift; keep them in perspective. They will (should) be gone someday.

9. Marriage is not about finding the right person, but rather about *being* the right person. When your focus is on your own behaviors and the way you treat your spouse, it will not be long before things begin to change.

10. Help your spouse to become more like Christ. The key to a happy marriage is not trying to control another person or force that person to do what you want; it is simply making yourself do what you should do in order to demonstrate love to the other person.

11. My wife and I purposely never mentioned or even said the word "divorce" (in regard to each other) in our thirty years together. It was never an option, and therefore it was never used as a threat. It was never something our children feared, even though they heard their own friends talk about it.

12. Become best friends before you're married, and stay best friends while you're married. Timothy Keller says, "Your marriage will slowly die if your spouse senses that he or she is not the first priority in your life. Buy only if your spouse is not just your lover and financial partner but your best friend is it possible for your marriage be your most important and fulfilling relationship." [50]

I hope you have gained some insights from these basic principles. I truly believe that you will struggle and maybe fail as you try to do any of these, apart from understanding and accepting the very first one. I know this only because I've tried and failed many times without standing on the truth of who I am in Christ. Some couples have found this truth, even not having heard this before from other marriage counselors. That is why I believe it is important to begin to understand the first principle if you are serious about developing healthy relationships.

Choose Today: Your Identity

Another learning experience that impacted my understanding of who I am in Christ was from a book by Larry Crabb. I was introduced to this truth while I was attending Moody Bible Institute. Crabb states, "God created us in His image, personal beings unlike all other creatures and like Him in our unique capacity for relationship. I understand the Scriptures to teach that relationships offer two elements that are absolutely essential if we are to live as God intended: (1) the security of being truly loved and accepted, and (2) the significance of making a substantial, lasting, positive impact on another person."[51] Crabb makes the case that if you are looking for your spouse, or anybody else for that matter, to find your own security or significance in in life, then you will ultimately be disappointed because others will let you down or are not able to meet your expectations. Why? Because your spouse, like you, is not perfect and is a sinner and therefore will sin. Our DNA causes us to look to self and protect our own selfish interests. Larry Crabb goes on to say,

FIND YOUR TRUE IDENTITY IN CHRIST

> Christ has made me secure and significant. Whether I feel it or not, it is true. I am instructed by God to believe that my needs are already met and therefore I am to live selflessly, concerned only with the needs of others. *The more I choose to live according to the truth of what Christ as done for me, the more I will come to sense the reality of my security and significance in Him.*[52]

You cannot change or control your spouse, but you can change you and your understanding of your identity!

Here are a few truths about all who have put their faith in Christ and therefore become God's children:

- Knowing our true identity in Christ creates a deep awareness of the truth that there isn't any condemnation for those who are in Christ (Romans 8:1).
- Knowing our true identity provides a vital benefit: it enables us to live with a Christ-consciousness instead of a sin consciousness (Hebrews 10:1–3, 14).
- Trusting who you are in Christ is essential to being confident that there is nothing more you have to prove as a child of the King (see attached list at the end of the chapter).
- We are told to be aware that our spiritual identity as:
  - "sons of God" (Galatians. 3:26)
  - "children of God" (John 1:12; 1 John 3:10)
  - "saints" (Romans. 8:27; Ephesians 1:18; 4:12)
  - "godly" (2 Peter. 2:9)
  - "righteous" (Ephesians 4:24; 2 Corinthians 5:21)
  - "perfect" (Philippians 3:15; Hebrews 12:23)
- "Yet to all who receive him, to those who believed in his name, he gave the right to become children of God" (John 1:12).
- "You are all sons of God through faith in Christ Jesus" (Galatians 3:26).
- "How great is the love the Father has lavished on us, that we should be called children of God! And that is what we are!" (1 John 3:1).

Steve McVey in his book *Grace Walk* says, "Understanding our identity is absolutely essential to our success in living the Christian life. No person can consistently behave in a way that is inconsistent with the way he perceives himself. Next to a knowledge of God, a knowledge of who we are is by far the most important truth we can possess."[53] Because our position and identity is found in Christ and our security and significance is only found in Him, then we are free to love our spouse with Christ's love, grace, mercy, and forgiveness. The reality of our security in Christ is seen in the fact that our salvation is a present possession that we must choose (Ephesians 1:3–8, 2:1–9, 4:32). Our salvation is something of which we can have complete assurance (1 Thessalonians 1:5, Colossians 2:2). The security of our marriage is a wonderful byproduct of our identity in Christ as a child of our Heavenly Father.

Choose Today...Each and Every Day

There's a story about the only survivor of a shipwreck. He washed up on a small, unoccupied island. He prayed for God to rescue him, and every day he scanned the horizon for help, but none seemed to be coming. He eventually managed to build a little hut out of driftwood to protect him from the elements and to store his few possessions. But then one day, after searching for food, he arrived home to find his little hut in flames, the smoke rolling up to the sky. Everything was lost. He was hurt with grief and anger: "God! How could you do this to me!"

Early the next day he was awakened by the sound of a ship approaching the island. It had come to rescue him.

"How did you know I was here?" the weary man asked his rescuers.

They replied, "We saw your smoke signal."

God always sees and knows what is going on in your life each and every day. He always wants to be with you and will always love you. Remember, it is only out of His love for us that we can love Him (1 John 1:9). Knowing that makes it possible to love Him with your entire life. Jesus clearly states that through what is called the Great Commandment. Jesus says: "'Love the Lord your God with all your heart and with all your soul and with all your mind.' This is the first and greatest commandment. And the second is like it: 'Love your neighbor as yourself'" (Matthew 22:37–39).

You might have thought or said the following at times: "I don't understand what is happening. I have asked God to use my life, and I really meant it. But it seems like the more I try to do what He wants me to do, the harder things become." Have you ever felt this way? Remember the Dann Spader quote I mentioned before: "The Christian life is impossible—you can't live it. But the Christian life is simple—it's Christ living through you." It is really important to know that *you* can't live the Christian life, only Christ can. That truth must ring loud and clear when beginning to understand "who we are in Christ." When we come to the end of ourselves, then we will be at a place where God can begin to influence and fill our hearts and minds.

So here's what I want you to do, with God helping you: Take your everyday, ordinary life—your sleeping, eating, going-to-work, and walking-around life—and place it before God as an offering. Embracing what God does for you is the best thing you can do for Him. Don't become so well adjusted to your culture that you fit into it without even thinking. Instead, fix your attention on God. You'll be changed from the inside out. (See Romans 12:1–2, MSG.)

I've read several books over the years about who we are in Christ that have been tremendously beneficial to me. Here are just a few highlights from some of those books:

Ed Gungor in his book *Religiously Transmitted Diseases*,

Whenever we make our life about self, we miss the mark. Acting for God was never part of the program. God never created people to be performers—acting independently of a direct connection with Him. We believe a lie when we think God is asking us to perform. It is also a lie that we can act perfect and take care of ourselves. Humans need God—we were created that way. There is grave danger in preaching a message of human performance. Such a sermon contends that there is something we can do to procure God's presence and favor in our lives. Doing good things somehow earns God. The problem is, God is not for sale. He only gives Himself to us.[54]

In *Grace Walks*, Steve McVey says,

In the spiritual world, trying harder is detrimental. Trying harder will defeat you every time. A person does not experience victory in the Christian life by trying hard to live for God. It just won't work! When Christians try to live by the rules, the outcome will be the same as it has always been. They will discover that they just can't measure up, regardless of how hard they try. The law is intended to make people realize, "I just can't do it. I've tried and tried, but I just can't live a successful Christian life." If that's how you feel, then you might be closer than you know to enjoying success. Your sense of failure may be the catalyst God wants to use to bring you to a new understanding of the meaning of the Christian life.[55]

The Apostle Paul puts it best when he says Christianity starts from God, it only works through God, and it ends up going back to God: "For from him and through him and to him are all things. To him be the glory forever!" (Romans 11:36).

Founder and President of Freedom in Christ Ministries Neil Anderson states, "The more you reaffirm who you are in Christ, the more your behavior will begin to reflect your true identity!"[56] It is not your striving that releases Christ's life through you. It is your trusting. God will gladly take the initiative of this journey at your invitation. Ask him to begin to reveal to you how much he loves you, and he will gladly take it from there.

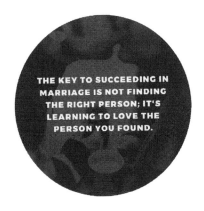

THE KEY TO SUCCEEDING IN MARRIAGE IS NOT FINDING THE RIGHT PERSON; IT'S LEARNING TO LOVE THE PERSON YOU FOUND.

Recounting Real Relationships

(This is a family that I know, but they have requested to remain anonymous)

Does divorce affect more than just the married couple? You bet it does! When it comes to divorce, the biggest fallacy is that kids are not affected and are resilient! They are definitely *not* resilient! As a child of divorced parents, I can attest to this firsthand.

When I was six years old, my mother and father bought and owned a resort on a lake in Northern Wisconsin. Because this was a summer resort only, my dad kept his business in Illinois and traveled back and forth every weekend. The stress of the situation became too much for my dad, and due to some other health problems, when I was nine years old, he had several severe strokes that left him paralyzed on one side as well as affected his speech.

Life changed drastically! He sold his business in Illinois and lived full time at our home on the resort. While most might think this was a good thing, my dad was full of resentment and anger, and the relationship between him and my mom worsened very quickly. He became violent and abusive in spite of his condition. The doctors said this was a normal response in a marriage that was shaky to begin with, which I soon found out to be the case. I witnessed violence in the form of screaming, door slamming, and food throwing, and at one point my father tried to run my mother down with our car as she and I walked across a bridge on our resort. I jumped off the side of the bridge into the gully, as did my mom, to avoid being hit. At a precious age from nine to twelve, I witnessed more heartbreak than any child should have to bear!

I thought that was how a marriage functioned. By the time I was fourteen, my mom and dad got divorced. My dad went back to live in Illinois. My mom sold the resort and soon after met a man and fell in love. Although he was a severe alcoholic, it didn't bother my mom, as she liked to drink too. Soon they were married, and now I had two stepsisters who lived with us. After about a year, my parents began to fight and argue, just as I had seen my mom and dad do. Within two years, they were divorced. They couldn't stand to be apart, but couldn't live together, and all in all, they married and divorced three times. All the while, I was learning this was the answer for a problematic relationship!

Because I witnessed my parents drinking and fighting while I was growing up, I thought this was the norm. I thought drinking and fighting was the way to live life, and so not only did I have no parental support in any aspect of my life, but I followed directly in their footsteps. As a teenager I partied like there was no tomorrow and had no respect for anyone or anything! I even thought that the greatest "freak-out" in life would be a head-on collision with a semi when I was wasted! Fortunately, God didn't think so, and knowing what my future would entail, He kept me from making that awful mistake! But heavy-duty partying was my life, and I not only drank and did drugs, but I was very salacious, because I didn't know how to have a lasting relationship with a guy. So I "dated" many, many guys always looking for "love," whatever that meant!

Then one day, at the age of twenty-six, I met a guy who truly did love me. But he had been married before and had two children already, so I was reluctant to go forward with the relationship. The one time I actually had a guy who wanted me for who I was, I resisted, because all I ever wanted in my life was a "normal" family. Normal to me meant husband and wife, married forever with no prior marriage or commitments. Getting involved with this guy meant starting out against my dream of having a family unit that was whole and intact. At the same time, I related to stepfamilies and chaos when it came to dealing with an "ex," from watching my mom handle her past relationships. I hated the fact that I could relate and that if I wanted this guy who loved me, that's what I had to do.

So I stepped into the relationship with both feet and with the attitude that if it didn't work out, I would just get divorced! It was the way, it was right, and it was okay to think that. Needless to say, as arguments came up my first instinct was always to leave. This seemed like a perfectly fine answer to me; however, he always managed to convince me to stay. At the age of twenty-nine, after being married for a year and a half, I found out I was pregnant. Suddenly I realized how much I loved and adored this baby, more than life itself, and that no matter what it took within me, there was *no way* I was going to put my child through what I had been through myself, D-I-V-O-R-C-E. Along the way, it wasn't as easy as I thought it would be. With every disagreement, my answer was to leave him. But then I pictured my baby girl growing up the way I did…and I couldn't do that to her.

Then along came my son, four and a half years later. Now I had two depending on me. As things got rough with his ex, problems increased with his first children, and there were fights between us, I dreamed more and more of leaving. This solution for a way out was so ingrained in my mind that I soon lived for the day that my youngest was eighteen and I could be free! But until then, I did *everything* possible to make it work for the sake of my children.

Then I realized the plans God had for me. In 2004, while attending a church service at a local church, I became saved by the blood and power of Jesus! It was amazing the way God how saved me from the act of divorce over and over and over again. Each time I was close to leaving, He literally stopped me! One time after we had a horrific fight and I was planning to leave the next day, I prayed that if God really wanted me to stay, He would put up a wall so I couldn't. That night I rolled my car, and when I landed, I was directly facing a wall of snow. I asked Him if it was "my wall," and He affirmed! In every incident, the good Lord had stopped me! Now our youngest is nineteen, we are "empty nesters," and we are still together. I have decided that we are the generation that will break the chain of divorce and that we will stay together until God takes one or both of us home. Our children will *not* be children of divorce, no matter how old they are!

Journey Together
Marriage Workbook

1) Christian activist Corrie ten Boom who helped Jews escape the Nazi Holocaust during World War II said, "Never be afraid to trust an unknown future to a known God." Why is it so hard to trust the unknown in our life to a God who knows everything that is going on in your life?

_____

_____

_____

2) Discuss what these words mean for you: "We saw how powerless we were to help ourselves; but that was good, for we put everything into the hands of God who alone could save us" (2 Corinthians 1:9). It is when we come to the end of ourselves, the end of trying harder, that God can begin His work. How might you begin to put everything into His hands?

_____

_____

_____

3) "The Christian life is impossible—you can't do it. But the Christian life is simple—it's Christ living through you," As I mentioned in this chapter this saying from Dann Spader, the founder of Sonlife Ministries, began a life-long journey that drastically changed my life. How might this truth be lived out in your life right now?

_____

_____

_____

4) Galatians 2:20 says, "I have been crucified with Christ and I no longer live, but Christ lives in me. The life I live in the body, I live by faith in the Son of God, who loved me and gave himself for me." Paul's life was completely changed by God's grace, and he understood that it is Christ who lived in and

through him. Do you believe that Christ is living in you, influencing your actions and thoughts, or do you still find yourself living your life in your own strength and power?

_____

_____

_____

5) Practically speaking, what does it look like to "be crucified with Christ and live by faith?" What are the places in your life where you forget that you have been crucified with Christ? Why do you think those places in particular give you spiritual unrest? God began this process, and He will complete it if you allow Him (Philippians 1:6). Take time with God every day this week to ask Him to help you understand and live out Galatians 2:20.

_____

_____

_____

6) What does it mean to you that, having put your faith in Christ, you are complete in Christ, and God has given you everything you need for life? (Colossians 2:10; 2 Peter 1:3)

_____

_____

_____

7) Go back through the twelve basic principles that can help create a healthy marriage (page 71-72) and discuss any that you agree with or any that you might be struggling with. Do you want to list other principles for you own marriage?

_____

_____

_____

8) I quoted Dr. Larry Crabb in this chapter from his book *The Marriage Builder* that he stated we need to find our security and significance in Christ alone. Why would looking to our spouse, our career, or anything else to find or fulfill our security and significance be a problem?

_____

_____

_____

9) As discussed in this chapter, Neil Anderson in several books he has written says, "The more you reaffirm who you are in Christ, the more your behavior will begin to reflect your true identity." Why would knowing our identity is found in Christ alone change our behavior?

_____

_____

_____

PRAY

Here is a prayer to get you started, and remember: it's not the words that matter so much as what's in your heart. Pray this prayer to begin to live a life in Christ alone. Read it out loud:

Lord, Your Holy Spirit is showing me this truth. I embrace it by faith, just as I embraced Jesus for me by faith and experienced forgiveness of my sins (Colossians 2:6). I now embrace Jesus in me as my life. Teach me of this truth by the Holy Spirit, so that I won't be captive any longer to trying to produce the life through my own efforts. In Jesus's name, Amen.

WHO I AM IN CHRIST[57]

I am Accepted in Christ

John 1:12	I am God's child
John 15:15	I am Christ's friend
Romans 5:1	I have been justified
1 Corinthians 6:17	I am united with the Lord and one with Him in spirit
1 Corinthians 6:20	I have been bought with a price, I belong to God
1 Corinthians 12:27	I am a member of Christ's body
Ephesians 1:1	I am a saint
Ephesians 1:5	I have been adopted as God's child
Ephesians 2:18	I have direct access to God through the Holy Spirit
Colossians 1:14	I have been redeemed and forgiven of all my sins
Colossians 2:10	I am complete in Christ

I am Secure in Christ

Romans 8:1-2	I am free forever from condemnation
Romans 8:28	I am assured that all things work together for good
Romans 8:33-34	I am free from any condemning charges against me
Romans 8:35	I cannot be separated from the love of God
2 Corinthians 1:21	I have been established anointed and sealed by God
Colossians 3:3	I am hidden with Christ in God
Philippians 1:6	I am confident that the good work God has begun in me will be perfected
Philippian 3:20	I am a citizen of heaven
2 Timothy 1:7	I have not been given a spirit of fear but of power love and a sound mind
Hebrews 4:16	I can find grace and mercy in time of need
1 John 5:18	I am born of God and the evil one cannot touch me

I Am Significant in Christ

Matthew 5:13-14	I am the salt and light of the earth
John 15:1,5	I am a branch of the true vine, a channel of His life
John 15:16	I have been chosen and appointed to bear fruit
Acts 1:8	I am a personal witness of Christ's
1 Corinthians 3:16	I am God's temple
2 Corinthians 5:17-20	I am a minister of reconciliation
2 Corinthians 6:1	I am God's co-worker
Ephesians 2:6	I am seated with Christ in the heavenly realm
Ephesians 2:10	I am God's workmanship
Ephesians 3:12	I may approach God with freedom and confidence
Philippians 4:13	I can do all things through Christ who strengthens me

REFERENCES

1. "32 Shocking Divorce Statistics", McKinley Irvin Family Law, October 30, 2012, www.mckinleyirvin. com/Family-Law-Blog/2012/October/32-Shocking-Divorce-Statistics.aspx

2. Brent A. Barlow, *Marriage Crossroads: Why Divorce is Often Not the Best Option* (Provo, Utah: Brigham Young University, 2003), page 24.

3. H. Norman Wright and Wes Roberts, *Before You Say "I Do": A Marriage Preparation Manual for Couples* (Eugene, Oregon: Harvest House Publishers, 1970)

4. Timothy Keller, The Meaning of Marriage (New York, New York: Penguin Group, 2011) page 89.

5. Brent A. Barlow, *Marriage Crossroads: Why Divorce is Often Not the Best Option* (Provo, Utah: Brigham Young University, 2003), page 22.

6. Susan Sparks, *Laugh Your Way to Grace: Reclaiming the Spiritual Power of Humor* (Woodstock, Vermont: Skylight Paths, 2010)

7. "Mark Twain Quotes", Mark Twain, www.brainyquote.com/quotes/quotes/m/marktwain100621. html

8. "The Extraordinary Importance of First Impressions", Sean M. Horan Ph.D., October 18, 2014, www.psychologytoday.com/blog/adventures-in-dating/201410/the-extraordinary-importance-first-impressions

9. "Law Firm Claims As Many As 20% Of Modern Divorces Cite Facebook In Filings", Kim LaCapria, December 22, 2009, www.inquisitr.com/53414/facebook-divorce-rate/

10. The Love Dare, www.thelovedarebook.com

11. Tony Evans, Marriage Matters (Chicago, IL: Moddy Publishers, 2010), page 32.

12. "Marriage Is a Battle . . . But Not Against Each Other", Greg Smalley, 2016, www.focusonthefamily. com/marriage/communication-and-conflict/marriage-is-a-battle-but-not-against-each-other

13. "In Defense of Marriage—Part 1", S. Michael Craven, July 23, 2008, www.christianpost.com/news/in-defense-of-marriage-part-i-33435/

14. "The Decline of a Nation", Kerby Anderson/ Probe Ministries, 1991, http://www.leaderu.com/orgs/probe/docs/decline.html

15. "Family If Things Go Well With", Michael Novak, http://www.inspirational-quotes-hq.com/Quote-On-Family-l002.html

16. "The Decline of a Nation", Kerby Anderson/ Probe Ministries, 1991, http://www.leaderu.com/orgs/probe/docs/decline.html

17. Glenn T. Stanton, *Why Marriage Matters* (Carol Stream, IL; NavePress, 1997), page 85.

18. "Marriage Quotes" , Darlene Schacht, October 4, 2013, www.timewarpwife.com/marriage-quotes/

19. Fireproof Movie, www.fireproofthemovie.com

20. Brent A. Barlow, Marriage Crossroads: Why Divorce is Often Not the Best Option (Provo, Utah: Brigham Young University, 2003), page 22

21. "Knowing Facts Still Matters (Even In An Age Of Wikipedia), Scott H. Young, December 2014, www.scotthyoung.com/blog/2014/12/08/knowing-facts-matters/

22. "Marriage in America: A Report to the Nation. Institute for American Values", Council on Families Institute for American Values, 1995, page 1.

23. Bridget Maher, *Deterring Divorce* (Family Research Council, 2004), page 6.

24. "How Much Will My Divorce Cost and How Long Will it Take?", Kathleen Michon, J.D., 2014, www.nolo.com/legal-encyclopedia/ctp/cost-of-divorce

25. "The Effects of Divorce on America", Patrick Fagan and Robert Rector/The Heritage Foundation, 2000, www.heritage.org/marriage-and-family/report/the-effects-divorce-america

26. Bridget Maher, *Deterring Divorce* (Family Research Council, 2004), page 10.

27. Amy Desai, *Should I Get A Divorce?: Things You Should Know Before You Call the Attorney*, 2006. Page 7.

28. Amy Desai, *Should I Get I Get A Divorce?: Things You Should Know Before You Call the Attorney*, 2006. Page 11.

29. "Abandonment", March 206 www.goodtherapy.org/learn-about-therapy/issues/abandonment

30. "The Effects of Divorce on Children", Patrick F. Fagan and Aaron Churchill, January 11, 2012 http://downloads.frc.org/EF/EF12A22.pdf

31. Bridget Maher, Deterring Divorce (Family Research Council, 2004), page 8.

32. Mark Gungor, *Laugh Your Way to a Better Marriage* (New Orleans, Atria Books, 2008).

33. Gary L. Thomas, *Sacred Marriage: What If God Designed Marriage to Make Us Holy More Than to Make Us Happy?* (Grand Rapids, MI: Zondervan, 2015) page 11.

34. Brent A. Barlow, *Marriage Crossroads: Why Divorce is Often Not the Best Option* (Provo, Utah: Brigham Young University, 2003), page 22.

35. Gary Chapman, *The Five Love Languages* (Chicago, IL: Northfield Publishing, 1992) page 30.

36. Timothy Keller, *The Meaning of Marriage* (New York, New York: Penguin Group, 2011) page 38.

37. Timothy Keller, *The Meaning of Marriage* (New York, New York: Penguin Group, 2011) page 136.

38. Timothy Keller, *The Meaning of Marriage* (New York, New York: Penguin Group, 2011) page 138.

39. "Leadership Blind Spots", John Maxwell, September 22, 2015, www.johnmaxwell.com/blog/leadership-blind-spots

40. Timothy Keller, *The Meaning of Marriage* (New York, New York: Penguin Group, 2011) page 147.

41. Timothy Keller, *The Meaning of Marriage* (New York, New York: Penguin Group, 2011) page 163.

42. John Piper, *Desiring God* (Colorado Springs, Colorado: Multnomah Books, 2011) page 119.

43. Timothy Keller, *The Meaning of Marriage* (New York, New York: Penguin Group, 2011) page 121.

44. "How You Love Differently When You're a Child of Divorce," Anna Bashedly, February, 2016 www.annabash.com/blog

45. Randy Alcorn, The Grace And Truth Paradox (Colorado Springs, Colorado: Multnomah Books, 2003)

46. Timothy Keller, *Every Good Endeavor: Connecting Your Work to God's Work* (New York, New York: Penguin Group, 2012) page 160.

47. Larry Osborne, *Ten Dumb Things Smart Christians Believe* (Colorado Springs, Colorado: Multnomah Books, 2010) page 12

48. Larry Osborne, Sermon: Can Faith Really Save Us? (North Coast Church January 2010) www.north-coastchurch.com/sermons/sermon-archive/

49. Plump, Wendy, "A Roomful of Yearning and Regret," The New York Times, December 9, 2010: Page ST6, www.nytimes.com/2010/12/12/fashion/12Modern.html

50. Timothy Keller, *The Meaning of Marriage* (New York, New York: Penguin Group, 2011) page 126.

51. Larry Crabb, *The Marriage Builder* (Grand Rapids, Michigan: Zondervan Publishing House, 1982) page 20.

52. Larry Crabb, *The Marriage Builder* (Grand Rapids, Michigan: Zondervan Publishing House, 1982) page 21.

53. Steve McVey, *Grace Walk* (Eugene, Oregon: Harvest House Publishers, 1995) page 42.

54. Ed Gungor, *Religiously Transmitted Diseases* (USA: Nelson Books, 2006) page 19.

55. Steve McVey, *Grace Walk* (Eugene, Oregon: Harvest House Publishers, 1995) page 18.

56. Neil Anderson, *Victory Over the Darkness* (Ventura, California, Regal Books, 1990) page 44.

57. Neil Anderson, *Victory Over the Darkness* (Ventura, California, Regal Books, 1990) page 31.

52800512R00059

Made in the USA
San Bernardino, CA
30 August 2017